UNDERSTANDING
BETH HENLEY

Understanding Contemporary American Literature
Matthew J. Bruccoli, Series Editor

Volumes on

Edward Albee • Sherman Alexie • Nicholson Baker
John Barth • Donald Barthelme
The Beats • The Black Mountain Poets • Robert Bly
Raymond Carver • Fred Chappell • Chicano Literature
Contemporary American Drama
Contemporary American Horror Fiction
Contemporary American Literary Theory
Contemporary American Science Fiction, 1926–1970
Contemporary American Science Fiction, 1970–2000
Contemporary Chicana Literature
Robert Coover • James Dickey • E. L. Doctorow • Rita Dove
John Gardner • George Garrett • John Hawkes • Joseph Heller
Lillian Hellman • Beth Henley • John Irving
Randall Jarrell • Charles Johnson • Adrienne Kennedy
William Kennedy • Jack Kerouac • Ursula K. Le Guin
Denise Levertov • Bernard Malamud
Bobbie Ann Mason • Jill McCorkle • Carson McCullers
W. S. Merwin • Arthur Miller • Toni Morrison's Fiction
Vladimir Nabokov • Gloria Naylor • Joyce Carol Oates
Tim O'Brien • Flannery O'Connor • Cynthia Ozick
Walker Percy • Katherine Anne Porter • Richard Powers
Reynolds Price • Annie Proulx • Thomas Pynchon
Theodore Roethke • Philip Roth • May Sarton • Hubert Selby, Jr.
Mary Lee Settle • Neil Simon • Isaac Bashevis Singer
Jane Smiley • Gary Snyder • William Stafford
Anne Tyler • Kurt Vonnegut • David Foster Wallace
Robert Penn Warren • James Welch • Eudora Welty
Tennessee Williams • August Wilson

UNDERSTANDING BETH HENLEY

Robert J. Andreach

University of South Carolina Press

Published in Columbia, South Carolina,
by the University of South Carolina Press

www.sc.edu/uscpress

Manufactured in the United States of America

13 12 11 10 09 08 07 06 8 7 6 5 4 3 2 1

Library of Congress Cataloging-in-Publication Data

Andreach, Robert J.
Understanding Beth Henley / Robert J. Andreach.
p. cm. — (Understanding contemporary American literature)
Includes bibliographical references and index.
ISBN-13: 978-1-57003-639-2 (cloth : alk. paper)
ISBN-10: 1-57003-639-X (cloth : alk. paper)
1. Henley, Beth—Criticism and interpretation. 2. Women and literature—United States—History—20th century. I. Title. II. Series.
PS3558.E4962Z525 2002
812'.54—dc22

2006005141

For my brothers Jim (in memoriam) and George
and my sisters-in-law Mary and Elaine

Contents

Series Editor's Preface

The volumes of *Understanding Contemporary American Literature* have been planned as guides or companions for students as well as good nonacademic readers. The editor and publisher perceive a need for these volumes because much of the influential contemporary literature makes special demands. Uninitiated readers encounter difficulty in approaching works that depart from the traditional forms and techniques of prose and poetry. Literature relies on conventions, but the conventions keep evolving; new writers form their own conventions—which in time may become familiar. Put simply, *UCAL* provides instruction in how to read certain contemporary writers—identifying and explicating their material, themes, use of language, point of view, structures, symbolism, and responses to experience.

The word *understanding* in the titles was deliberately chosen. Many willing readers lack an adequate understanding of how contemporary literature works; that is, what the author is attempting to express and the means by which it is conveyed. Although the criticism and analysis in the series have been aimed at a level of general accessibility, these introductory volumes are meant to be applied in conjunction with the works they cover. They do not provide a substitute for the works and authors they introduce, but rather prepare the reader for more profitable literary experiences.

M. J. B.

Acknowledgments

For permission to reprint, in rewritten form, two articles, I want to thank *Notes on Contemporary Literature* for Robert J. Andreach, "A Fusing Allusion in Beth Henley's *L-Play*," 34, no. 4 (September 2004): 6–8. Copyright © 2004 by William S. Doxey; and the *Southern Quarterly* for Robert J. Andreach, "The Missing Five Years and Subjectivity in Beth Henley's *Abundance*," 39, no. 3 (Spring 2001): 141–50. Copyright © 2001 by the University of Southern Mississippi. Reproduced by permission.

I also want to thank John Greene and John Stibravy, two friends and former colleagues, for sharing resources and assisting in the manuscript preparation.

Finally, I want to thank the staff of the University of South Carolina Press, especially Karen Beidel, for shepherding this book through the production process.

UNDERSTANDING
BETH HENLEY

CHAPTER 1

Introduction

Beth Henley's *Crimes of the Heart* was the co-winner in 1979 of the Great American Play Contest sponsored by the Actors Theatre of Louisville, where it had its world premiere. It subsequently moved to New York City in 1980 and to Broadway in 1981. In New York City it won the Pulitzer Prize for Drama, "the first play to win the prestigious award before opening on Broadway," and the New York Drama Critics Circle Award for Best New American Play. Performed within and without the United States, made into a motion picture, and anthologized, *Crimes of the Heart* marked for the playwright an auspicious beginning to the 1980s. Of her other five plays of that decade, one was made into a motion picture, two were anthologized, three had London productions, and all were staged in New York City, America's theater capital.[1]

Although some of Henley's six plays of the 1990s have been produced in cities such as Los Angeles and Chicago and in regional festivals in, for instance, Poughkeepsie, New York, and Stockbridge, Massachusetts, only two of the six—the first and the last—have had New York City productions. That something happened to Henley's visibility as a playwright was confirmed by Todd Haimes, artistic director of New York's Roundabout Theatre, the company that commissioned *Impossible Marriage*, Henley's last play of the 1990s: "Our intention was to commission plays by established playwrights, but perhaps playwrights who were not being produced as often as we'd like to see them produced. We came up with a list of playwrights that interested us who hadn't been seen recently in New York and Beth Henley happened to be at the top of the list."[2]

Frank Rich's review of the first play of the 1990s offers a likely explanation for what happened. While he praised *Abundance* as Henley's "most provocative play in years," he also faulted it for failing to realize its potential: "Though its ideological reach tries to extend to sexual, economic and racial warfare alike, the play seems small and scattershot, more like a patchwork quilt than a large, ingeniously conceived canvas that is all of a piece." He went on to give instances of its not being "all of a piece": "There are too many deadpan vignettes of equal length and dramatic weight, too many repetitions, too many prosaic transitions between time frames, too many endings to each act."[3] No one would criticize the plays that preceded it for not being "all of a piece"; as Rich reminded his readers, by the end of the decade the style that had captivated audiences with its freshness had become formulaic. Yet Henley's first play of the new decade, which opens in the Wyoming Territory of the 1860s and spans twenty-five years, is so episodic that its fragmentation would disorient audiences familiar with her plays of the 1980s, which focus on a day or two of small-town life in the Deep South. As if the fragmentation were not enough, Rich located another source of disorientation in the director's mode of production being at cross-purposes with the play's architectonics.

One can disagree with Rich by arguing that just such fragmentation, disorientation, and ambiguities are the play's strength, but his argument is understandable. While praising the play, he felt compelled to detail its departure from the kind of play the author's name would conjure in the potential theatergoer's mind.

Given the nature of a theater review, he could not pursue the implications of Henley's changed style. And even if he had, the two plays that follow *Abundance* have modes of production light years away from that of the Deep South plays. *Signature* is set in a futuristic Los Angeles; its mode of production "should be expressionistic."[4] The set of *Control Freaks* "should be a frightening combination of dream real, fake real, and real."[5] Thus the likely explanation for Henley's lack of current visibility is that *Abundance* ushered in a decade of works that departed from her earlier style so radically that she left behind the producers and audiences who had supported the earlier plays. She is, however, too important a theater artist and too central to the contemporary American theater to remain on the periphery of playwrights whose works receive major productions.

If the perception of Henley's theater is that her work of the 1990s is a radical departure, and a falling off, from that of the 1980s, the publication in 2000 of the two-volume collected edition of her plays should correct the perception, aptly summarized by Gary Richards, that the "thrilling fresh young voice of a wunderkind has given way to stridency, confusion, and even ineptitude, leaving high expectations more or less unfulfilled after an initial flash of brilliance."[6] Each of the volumes contains the plays of a decade: volume 1, the 1980s, and volume 2, the 1990s. There are departures in the second volume from the naturalistic mode of production in the first volume, but they reflect a change in the self-discovery that Henleyan characters experience. The self-discovery in five of the six plays of the 1980s gives the characters one sense of their worth that their culture denies: they are capable of loving and being loved. The self-discovery in *Abundance,* the one exception to the earlier decade's work, gives them another sense of worth: possessing imagination, they can be creative. The two plays immediately following *Abundance* endow Henley's characters with either the first or the second of these senses but not both, because the two discoveries conflict. They make competing appeals to the self; they engage the self differently. As Henley's work progresses during the 1990s, though, and the character who experiences the discovery begins to overcome self-doubt by drawing strength from the discovery, she or he explores the two engagements, interacting them in an attempt to reconcile them. The attempted reconciliation creates a new life, a new union with new possibilities, as the interaction of the naturalistic mode of production of the 1980s and the experimental modes of the 1990s creates a new theater with new possibilities. For the critic who begins at the beginning and studies the departures and discoveries, the interaction and the attempted reconciliation, all of Henley's plays are "of a piece."

The production of *Impossible Marriage* in 1998, Henley's sixth play of the 1990s and the second of the decade to be produced in New York City, made clear that *Abundance* was not a digression but the beginning of a decade of experimentation. The publication in 2000 of the two-volume collected edition brought together these two plays with the decade's four middle plays—*Signature, Control Freaks, Revelers,* and *L-Play*—plays that had not been produced in New York City and about which no journal articles had been written. The publication therefore invited a study of the continuity running not only throughout each decade but also throughout the collected works, for although the plays of the 1990s depart from Henley's earlier work in mode of production and in style and tone, they develop themes, motifs, and images at work in the plays of the 1980s.

Critical studies of the plays of the second decade, individually or collectively, were not immediately forthcoming, however.

None were listed in the annual bibliography that the journal *Modern Drama* published through 1999. In 2003 an Internet search of the *MLA Bibliography* for the years 1999–2003 yielded a total of seven items, one of which was my article on *Abundance*. Five of the other six—articles in journals, a dissertation abstract, and sections of books—address issues in plays of the first decade. The sixth, written by a major contributor to Henley scholarship, Karen L. Laughlin, does refer to the later plays, but this six-page entry in a history of southern women's literature cannot go into them in depth.[7] *Beth Henley: A Casebook* appeared in 2002. Of its seven sections, only one is devoted exclusively to the plays of the 1990s, although three of the decade's plays are examined in depth in the book. As the volume's editor, Julia A. Fesmire, assesses the state of Henley scholarship, it "is, until now, somewhat limited. Quite a few newspaper and magazine articles and reviews of her films and various productions of her plays (including the later ones) have been published, along with several interviews with the playwright herself, but there are no full length studies of her oeuvre and surprisingly few scholarly articles."[8]

This book studies her oeuvre. For example, the final three plays of the 1990s can be seen as a trilogy, an achievement in its own right. In the 1980s it was easy to think of Henley as a playwright whose southern sensibility so informed her theater that she did not connect with any other styles.[9] Her sensibility is distinctly hers, but plays of the 1990s do connect with traditions outside the South. The title alone of the first of the trilogy's plays should resonate for anyone familiar with the history of Western drama. *Revelers* (named with other plays in one sentence in one of the seven sections of the *Casebook*) takes place on the grounds of a northern Wisconsin cottage, where colleagues gather to honor with a memorial service the recently deceased founder of a theater. He is present in the form of a "*life-size cutout replica . . . with blazing eyes, sensual sneering lips, and a thin pale wolflike face.*" Inside the cottage masks and other objects associated with theater surround the replica. To signal the start of the service, a revelry that the founder requested in his last wishes, his colleagues bring the figure outside to the makeshift stage, where the "innovative genius"[10] comes to life in his followers until the final scene celebrates the mystery of death in life and life in death. Yet according to the collected edition and the *Casebook, Revelers* has had only two productions: one by the New York Stage and Film Company in Poughkeepsie, New York, and one by the Center Theater in Chicago.

The critic who hears the opening line of *The Waste Land* in *Revelers* should not be surprised that Eliot's poetry is more strongly present in the second of the three plays that can be considered a trilogy. (When references to it are tallied, the play is accorded approximately one page in the *Casebook.*) *L-Play* is a play of fragments—but fragments that connect to form a quest to reconcile the two discoveries that make competing claims on the self: the discovery of the potential for love in the plays of the 1980s and the potential for creativity in those of the 1990s. For the third play, *Impossible Marriage* (accorded approximately one page in the *Casebook*), Henley confides in its introduction that she decided to write "something like *The Importance of Being Earnest,* except by me."[11] Although she does not identify a second source, a Chekhovian tone and style interacts with the play's Wildean tone and style. Internal evidence points to the influence of a specific play by the Russian playwright, whom she credited in an early interview with having influenced her "more than anyone else."[12] Within these competing influences, one of the characters quotes from Dylan Thomas's "Lament" while the setting and individual lines invoke *A Midsummer Night's Dream* and *Paradise Lost.* Creating theater in contemporary images, the trilogy dramatizes a modern quest to unify an absurd, fragmented universe that is realized artistically in the interaction of postmodern genres, styles, and tones with unconventional unions of traditionally conceived characters.

The three plays of the trilogy are the last to be studied. A one-act play, *Sisters of the Winter Madrigal,* was produced in 2001 and has been published, but it dates from early in Henley's career.[13] Two other plays, *Family Week* and *Exposed,* have also been produced but have not been published.

CHAPTER 2

1980s—Naturalistic Plays

Elizabeth Becker Henley, Becker being her mother's maiden name, was born May 8, 1952, in Jackson, Mississippi, and grew up there but left for an undergraduate degree at Southern Methodist University in Texas. She was a sophomore in 1972 when she wrote a one-act play for a playwriting class. The university did not awaken her theatrical interest: she had been fascinated by theater since she was a child attending rehearsals and watching her mother, an actress, perform in Jackson theaters. In 1974, her senior year, the university produced *Am I Blue* under the pseudonym she chose for herself, Amy Peach. In 1981 Connecticut's Hartford Stage Company presented the piece; the following year New York's Circle Repertory Company presented it as part of a triple bill. By the time of its New York staging, however, Henley had won the Pulitzer Prize for her first full-length play, *Crimes of the Heart,* written in 1978 in Los Angeles, where the playwright had moved after a year of graduate study in theater arts at the University of Illinois in 1975–1976. She had gone to the West Coast in the hope of building a career as an actress but instead found fame as a playwright, though not initially. She submitted the play to a few regional theater companies with no success. A friend submitted it to the Actors Theatre in Louisville, where it was staged and declared co-winner of a new American play contest before eventually opening in New York, first in an Off-Broadway production in 1980 and then in a Broadway production in 1981.

Though she was living in Los Angeles, Henley set her first two full-length plays in Mississippi towns. *Crimes of the Heart* takes place in Hazlehurst, the home of her father's family, and *The Miss Firecracker Contest* takes place in Brookhaven, the home of her mother's family. The other plays of the 1980s, including her initial one-act piece, are set in either Mississippi or neighboring Louisiana. The characters in these plays are outsiders at risk. Since by virtue of their nonconformity they are, in Colby H. Kullman's designation, "intentionally marginalized,"[1] they risk being unable to share their feelings, insights, and experiences with others because they are alone, punished for their difference. They risk being institutionally isolated in a prison or asylum because they are so alone, so outside behavioral norms, that their actions warrant their removal from society. The hope, on the other hand, is finding a kindred soul. *Am I Blue* incorporates the pattern of fulfilled hope in a rudimentary form. The play opens with an outsider seated alone. John Polk is joined by another outsider, Ashbe, who makes an overture of friendship, although it is tentative because by cloaking herself with his raincoat, she remains alone. Yet through talking, they discover themselves and the ways in which they subvert cultural expectations, so that by play's end they are a couple, dancing together.

Crimes of the Heart develops the one-act play's themes into a Pulitzer Prize–winning drama. Each of the three Magrath sisters violates cultural norms: Lenny by driving their socially conditioned cousin, Chick, from the house and by taking the initiative with a man, Meg by rebelling from her teenage years onward and by going for a moonlit ride with a married man, and Babe by having an affair with a black youth and by shooting her husband, Zackery. Each discovers herself during the course of the play. Lenny discovers that she is a person of worth who can have a loving relationship with a man; Meg, that she can care about someone; and Babe, that she is not insane and in danger of being put away—that she is therefore not alone.

These two plays also begin a process that continues through the plays of the 1980s of dramatizing naturalistically the relationship between the interior self and the exterior world. Since the outsider strives to draw strength from within herself or himself, submitting to a culture that denies, deprecates, or represses interiority threatens the self's vitality. Conversely, isolation threatens the self's development because the outsider needs interaction with the world to test herself or himself. This need explains why the threat of exclusion, whether imposed by the self or society, is so grave a danger to one's well-being. Told by Zackery that he will have her confined in an institution, Babe attempts to commit suicide as Mrs. Magrath did. The comedy that delights in the unexpected thwarts the attempt—actually two attempts. Since her mother hanged herself, Babe attempts the same, but the rope breaks, sending her into the kitchen and into the oven. Gaining insight into her mother's final act, this time she tries to abort the suicide by removing her head from the oven, only to hit her head and fall back into it; Meg has to rescue her. The play ends with the three sisters sharing a "*magical*"[2] moment as they celebrate Lenny's birthday. The intentionally marginalized can reconcile the pressures from within and without the self so long as there are others with whom to share magical moments.

In her study of Henley's first three full-length plays—*Crimes of the Heart, The Miss Firecracker Contest,* and *The Wake of Jamey Foster*—Nancy D. Hargrove finds "in the closing scene" of each the "powerful force of human solidarity." One of the first authors to study Henley, Hargrove also makes the connection that my own study does. She writes that "perhaps the dominant theme of her drama ultimately is the value of love, with family love providing this support more often than romantic love. Further, although they are flawed human beings, the major characters learn something valuable about themselves or their world in the process of the drama."[3] The first sentence, no "perhaps" about it, describes the dominant theme of the plays of the 1980s, and it is so because of the second sentence. The self-discovery the characters experience is that they are capable of loving and being loved. The epiphany—the self-recognition—is a cause for celebration because their culture denies them a spiritual reality. Their culture perceives them naturalistically.

The term *naturalism* is crucial to understanding Henley's theater. The first meaning refers to a conception of humankind. "The fundamental view of man which the naturalist takes is of an animal in the natural world, responding to environmental forces and internal stresses and drives, over none of which he has either control or full knowledge."[4] The character conception in *Am I Blue* lacks impact as an instance of such naturalism because the characters, driven as they are by needs they do not fully comprehend, are typical for their ages. John Polk is seventeen, and Ashbe is sixteen. A better instance of naturalism is Henley's selection of the play's environment. It opens in a bar in the French Quarter of New Orleans. When told to leave because they are underage, the two teenagers pass through a seedy street, where a barker, "*perhaps . . . accompanied by a whore,*" tries to entice them into his establishment and a drunken bum falls near them and vomits. When they arrive at Ashbe's home, it is described as a "*run-down apartment in a run-down apartment house.*"[5] The character conception in *Crimes of the Heart* also is a better instance. When Doc, now married, whom Meg abandoned years earlier, asks why she no longer sings professionally, she says, "I don't know," going on to tell him that she went insane and was put in a psychiatric ward. When he then asks, "What happened?" she can only repeat, "I don't really know" (44). Although she does not allude to their mother's suicide as often as Babe does, the fear that they inherited their mother's mental instability is a specter haunting these two sisters. The shock of finding the mother's body drove Meg to steel herself against emotional involvements so as not to be a "weak person" (36) who might attempt suicide. Zackery's phone call threatening to have her declared insane and committed to an asylum provokes Babe to attempt suicide.

Oppressive environments, "sordid" (6) relationships—for that is cousin Chick's judgment of Meg's relationship with Doc years earlier—and characters who are helpless victims of forces over which they have no control and cannot understand imply a naturalistic view of existence. Henley is not a naturalist playwright according to this meaning of the term because the drama's action leads to an epiphanous scene in which the character discovers that she can understand herself and her situation and make choices accordingly. Yet the meaning is present in Henley's theater. The environments are oppressive because although the dominant culture perceives outsiders as having feelings, they are the instinctual drives and elemental passions that put them outside the culture's norms. The characters must therefore be controlled: broken and mastered. The deceased's brother in *The Wake of Jamey Foster* lifts his sister-in-law's sister's chin as he changes her name to his liking. "Lifting my chin up like that—you're making me feel like some sort of goddamn horse—I'm not a horse!" Collard resists him. Undeterred,

Wayne backs her against a chair. "You are a horse! A goddamn horse! Come here—come here—."[6]

Even though characters resist the oppression, they can be affected by how they are perceived. "I'm a shit. A hopeless shit!" (96) is Collard's self-perception before she experiences self-discovery. Hence the Henleyan conflict on the simplest level is between society's naturalistic perception of the outsider and the outsider's striving to overcome that perception without sacrificing individuality. An example in *Crimes of the Heart* is the exchange between socially conditioned Chick and Meg. When the latter lights a cigarette, the former reminds her that smoking causes cancer. Meg rebuffs her by telling her that flirting with death gives her a "sense of controlling" her "own destiny. What power!" she exclaims, offering her cousin a "drag." Lenny interrupts "*to break the tension*" (17). Because those who are intentionally marginalized struggle to resist the dominant culture's perception of them, the first meaning of naturalism—the deterministic meaning—does not apply to Henley's character conception but to other characters' perception within a play of a marginalized character, a perception that can affect that character's self-perception.

The second meaning of the term *naturalism* refers to a play's style or mode of production that attempts "to put on stage as exact a copy of life as possible, down to the smallest detail."[7] The stage directions for *Am I Blue* specify an apartment living room that is a "*malicious pig sty*" with objects "*thrown all about*" (74). The set of *Crimes of the Heart* is a kitchen with a telephone that rings, an oven into which Babe puts her head, and the ingredients—lemons, sugar, ice cubes—for making lemonade. The best evidence of this naturalism is in Henley's introduction to the second play. Knowing that the production could not afford a new birthday cake at every performance, she had the lights come down on the sisters before they cut pieces of it until a prop master designed a fake cake with a real section. She was delighted that the three actresses could "cut, eat, and smear cake every night" (ix). Because the mode of production that Henley espoused remained fairly constant throughout the decade of the 1980s, the plays of this decade are naturalistic in the second meaning of the term.

By attempting to put on stage in act 1 the living room of a house and in act 2 the dressing room for a carnival contest, *The Miss Firecracker Contest* exhibits this naturalism as well. The culture's perception of four of the characters is also naturalistic. Delmount, for example, was confined to an institution for a violent loss of control, though, he contends, unjustifiably so. To make matters worse, he could have been released after two months, but his sister, socially conditioned Elain, would not sign custody papers. Her refusal to accept her brother exemplifies society's method for controlling conformity. Society fails to break Delmount's spirit, however. More defiant than ever, he is one of the play's four nonconformists.

A nonconformist at heart, Carnelle spends much of the play trying to conform. Reared by her aunt, Delmount and Elain's mother, she compensated for a lack of "self-esteem" by sleeping with "every worthless soul in Brookhaven trying to prove she was attractive"[8] until she earned the reputation of Miss Hot Tamale. As she sees herself, that part of her life is in the past. In the present, as she explains to Elain, who returns to Brookhaven after leaving her husband, she has reformed: "I go to church now and I'm signed up to where I take an orphan home to dinner once a week or to a movie; and—and I work on the cancer drive here just like you do in Natchez" (157–58). Her future holds the promise of a new life if she can win the Miss Firecracker Contest as Elain once did, for then, she tells Delmount, "I would be able to leave this town in a crimson blaze of glory!" (163)

Since Carnelle's goal is creating a "new" self (181), winning the socially prestigious contest would be "visible proof" (168) that she has changed. Yet once the judges award her last place, despite a stupendous performance in the talent segment, she realizes the folly of trying to emulate Elain and her aunt in a town that will never let her forget that she was Miss Hot Tamale. "I can't believe I ever wanted to be like you or that mean old monkey either!" she says to her cousin, and then losing the control she has kept in check, she spits at all that the aunt represents as the standard bearer of Brookhaven's norms: "Die you monkey! Die!" She will not, however, evade the consequences of her decision to enter the contest. When Delmount tells her she does not have to walk behind the float in the parade, she replies, "Look, if you come in last, you follow that float. I took a chance and I came in last; so, by God, I'm gonna follow that float!!" (197). Realizing the folly of trying to be someone she is not while accepting responsibility for the someone she is prepares for her self-discovery. The epiphany in turn leads into the play's closing image, similar to that of *Crimes of the Heart*, with Carnelle sharing a magical moment with Delmount and Popeye, another of the play's nonconformists.

At this point, following a discussion of the first two full-length plays of the 1980s, the reader might expect an analysis of self-discovery in Henley's plays, but this analysis must be postponed because the self-discovery in *The Miss Firecracker Contest* is the one exception to these early plays mentioned in the introduction. Since it is the second of the two varieties of self-discoveries that Henleyan characters experience, it belongs with the analysis of the later plays. Parallels, however, can be drawn between the experiences in these two plays. The self-discovery—the epiphany or self-recognition—and the magical moment are separate but related experiences that overcome the naturalistic perception and self-perception in that they make the discoverer aware of a reality that she or he can share. The self-discovery precedes and makes possible the magical moment, which in turn validates or actualizes the discovery, for sharing the reality is the essence of the magical moment.

Henley does not deny the basis for the naturalistic perception. In an interview she admitted, "Well, humans are animals. We're mammals; I think we should stop pretending that we're not." But the animal is only half of human nature. The other half is spiritual, and it is the incompatibility, the "strange mixture," of "primitive instincts, intellect and spiritual confusion" that fascinates her. The patriarchal culture perceives only the animal half; through epiphany, a character discovers the spiritual half. And the magical moment, although she does not refer to it in the interview, reconciles the incompatibility. Even though "filled with dark, bloody, primitive urges and desires," the character not only can "seek love and kindness," she or he can actualize the love and kindness.[9]

Conformists can know themselves in Henley's imaginative world, but they do not discover a depth in themselves beneath the superficial self-knowledge that would create the magical moment. Elain wants to create a new self by leaving her husband and children in Natchez and declaring her independence in Brookhaven. But she cannot. Unable to forgo the creature comforts her husband provides, she lets him know she is ready to come home. Her one concession to nonconformity is spending an illicit evening with a partner she met at the contest before returning to respectability. His identity is an example of the ambiguity found throughout Henley's theater. Billy J. Harbin, Alan C. Shepard, and Larry G. Mapp,[10] among other critics, identify him as Mac Sam, one of Carnelle's former lovers, who sells balloons at the carnival. Described as "*extraordinarily sensual,*" he is also in "*drastically poor health*" (175)—not only because he has syphilis, given to him by Carnelle and for which he refuses to take the shots that will cure the disease, but because he has "TB, alcoholics disease, rotting gut. I tell ya," he explains to his former lover, "I'm having fun taking bets on which part of me'll decay first: the liver, the lungs, the stomach, or the brain" (202). Elain does not know he is disease ridden, and they are magnetically attracted to each other, but she is present when he has a coughing spell and Carnelle vents her humiliation over finishing last at him: "And why don't you get well!?! You make me *sick* you're so *sick*!! You look like shit!!!" (197). Apparently his appearance and ill health do not dull Elain's appetite.

When the assignation is viewed from Mac Sam's perspective, the ambiguity increases. One would think that a thirty-two-year-old "beauty" (145), an elegantly dressed socialite, and a former contest winner who is asked to give a speech on her life and who intends to be "reckless" under the "wisteria trees" (199) would be desirable to a thirty-six-year-old seller of balloons, but apparently she is not. He instead proposes an evening together to Carnelle. Were she to accept, he would be with her. She declines, at which time he reluctantly leaves for the "wisteria trees" (202). If Elain is waiting for him, Harbin's comment that Mac Sam is a "character so repugnant that Elain's action can only be attributed to lunacy or the author's antic whim"[11] has to be taken seriously. Incidentally, in the film version, for which Henley wrote the screenplay, the cousin leaves not with Mac Sam but with a contest dignitary. That in itself proves nothing about her choice in the play though, because Henley made changes in the script from stage to screen as she did with *Crimes of the Heart.*

Whoever her partner is, Elain returns to her husband: "I need someone who adores me" (194). Satisfied with what she can command and feeling no need to explore beyond the adoration, she does not experience self-discovery or a magical moment. Neither does Katty in *The Wake of Jamey Foster.* The wife of the deceased's brother has as much contempt for herself as her husband Wayne has for her: "I hate the me I have to be with him. If only I could have the baby it would give me someone to love and make someone who'd love me" (131). Humiliated after hearing Wayne's sexual advances to Collard, she flees to the bathroom and refuses to come out until the other women's confessions of their own humiliation draw her out. "To talk about our lives . . . [is] an important human need" (26), Meg explains to Babe in *Crimes of the Heart* to encourage her younger sister to talk about the circumstances that led to her shooting Zackery. Meg also figures in Babe's self-discovery. After pulling her sister's head out of the oven, Meg gets Babe to reveal the circumstances that led to the suicide attempt: Zackery's phone call to tell her he was having her committed to an asylum. The older sister convinces her that her husband cannot do that. "Why not?" she asks. "'Cause you're not insane," Meg answers (61). By the time Lenny arrives home, Babe has had her moment of self-discovery. She can say, "And I'm not like Mama. I'm not so all alone" (62), because she has two sisters with whom she can talk.

Talking about one's life does not guarantee self-discovery. Neither is it the sole activity that generates self-discovery. Lenny's chasing Chick out of the house after the cousin called Meg a "tramp" (57) emboldens the oldest sister to phone Charlie, whose desire to see her again is the basis of her discovery that she can have a loving relationship with a man. A chain of events—the plot or arrangement of incidents—leads to the self-discovery, but with each character who experiences such an cpiphany or self-recognition, talking about her or his life is part of the plot. Elain and Katty are exceptions in that they talk about their lives but do not experience self-discovery. Before Katty retires for the night, the widow, Marshael Foster, asks her what she intends to do about her situation with her womanizing husband. The wife answers, "Why, nothing. That's all I can do. I don't have children or a career like you do," she defends herself. "Anyway I don't like changes. My hair's still the same as I wore it in college" (131–32). She therefore forecloses any possibility of a self-discovery or magical moment—of discovering a love she can share.

Marshael is the character with whom Katty has to be compared. Not only did Jamey abandon Marshael for another woman, when she visited him in the hospital, the other woman, Esmerelda, was there and while she and Jamey talked, he held Esmerelda's hand or squeezed her waist. To add insult to injury, Esmerelda sends a pie with a condolence card to the wake. Yet by talking about the life she shared with her late husband, Marshael tries to understand what she felt for him. "It's like a hole's been shot through me, and all my insides have been blown out somewhere else," she confesses, adding, "I just wish I knew what I felt for Jamey. First one thing, I guess, and then another, I sure wish I knew. It haunts me not to know" (119–20). His leaving her for another woman and then dying have left her emotionally disoriented until talking to the other women, about the hospital humiliation to ease Katty's humiliation, and to herself takes her downstairs to a confrontation with the corpse. Her monologue contains three realizations, one or more of which constitute self-discovery in Henley's plays of the 1980s. Despite her rage at Jamey for abandoning her, she realizes she loved him because she needs to love and be loved. "I'm not . . . nothing," she fumes at the coffin. His death does not end her life; she knows she wants "something" from the life ahead of her (134).

This scene begins the self-discovery toward which all of Henley's plays move. Marshael's descent into the parlor where the dead body is displayed is a descent into the death of feeling within herself: the "hole" shot through her. The three realizations are an awakening of feeling. Knowing she can feel, knowing she is not dead, she runs from the house in her quest for the "something" she lacks. Her running serves two purposes. Since the confrontation with the corpse is the nadir of her descent, she has freed herself to experience elevating feelings, and her exiting the house frees Henley from dramatizing the interior discovery, which occurs offstage. Marshael does complete her self-discovery. When she appears the following morning, she is resolute in not attending the church service and she thinks she "can sleep" (137), as she has not been able to do for days. Furthermore, the play ends with a magical moment. Marshael laughs for the first time—and laughter is a component of the closing scenes of *Am I Blue, Crimes of the Heart,* and *The Miss Firecracker Contest* as well.

The character with whom she shares her magical moment is a would-be suitor, Brocker Slade, whose self-discovery runs parallel to hers. His arrival angers Marshael because he failed to respond to her emotional need the night he drove her home from the hospital. Not knowing what to do because theirs had never been a sexual relationship, and feeling that he would be taking advantage of her distraught state, he left her in the car after she told him to pull over and walked home. "Lordy, lord, is there no redemption in your heart?" he asks her. "It's in mighty short supply," she answers. "What do you want from me?" he then asks. "*It comes to her*" on the balcony: "Triumph! It's a feeling I'm sadly lacking. Give me some triumph: some glory: some exaltation!" (123)

His conception of exaltation, climbing the side of the house to take her to the moon, is ludicrous, for he falls to the ground as soon as he begins the ascent, eliciting her derision: "You stupid old fool" (123). Yet their words reverberate throughout the rest of the play. As she begins her monologue, she repeats his appeal to her: "I've got t' have something . . . redemption" (134). Just before she begins her monologue by her late husband's body, Brocker tells Marshael's brother how he failed her driving home from the hospital. Talking about his life makes him understand her disgust with him and his need to redeem himself, and he exits the house on his quest: "Exaltation! Love! Rapture! Glory! That's all there is! That's all that's left" (133). As she exits the house, he places a ladder against the house and ascends it, calling to his "Love" that he is taking her in his "arms to paradise" (134). But he is unaware that Marshael is outside the house and Collard is sleeping in her sister's bedroom because the gathering of family members for the wake necessitates doubling up. Were Collard not in the room, Brocker would still be committing a fundamental error. Pelted with eggs by Collard for disturbing her sleep, he descends to ground level and beyond, for he must spend the night in a ditch with his dog.

After spending the night with his dog, Brocker stinks. When Marshael tells him so the following morning, he apologizes, "Sorry. Look, I'll go change. I'll just go change" (138). He does change: his clothes and his approach to her. He does not abandon her as her husband did and as he did driving home from the hospital, but gives her a second chance. After the others leave for the church service, he positions himself on ground level beneath the bedroom and begins playing a song on his spoons. Having discovered the "something" she needs, love and forgiveness, Marshael comes out on the balcony and gives him a second chance as well by first asking him to get some Easter candy for her children and then asking him to play something for her. He does, his singing punctuated by her appreciation: "That's nice"; "That's a nice song"; "I like it"; and "I do" (140). Though the last utterance suggests the nuptial vow, what happens to Marshael and Brocker is left open, just as what happens to Babe and her lawyer Barnette is left open at the end of *Crimes of the Heart.* It is the openness that makes the difference, however, in whether or not a character can create a new life, and this openness is made possible by the discovery, in descent, of a real or true self, an interiority, buried beneath the culture's naturalistic perception and the character's attendant self-deprecation.

Marshael is also instrumental in Collard's self-discovery. The widow's sister is a variation on Carnelle in *The Miss Firecracker Contest,* a woman who compensates for low self-esteem by sleeping around. Collard even propositions Brocker, who declines because of his feelings for Marshael. "Are you really this tough?" he asks. Her reply illuminates the role-playing in which Henleyan characters engage: "No, darling, I'm pretending to be tough. But if you pretend really hard, it amounts to about the same thing" (122). By giving her responsibility,

Marshael enables her to free herself from her low self-esteem so that she does not have to pretend, but can be herself. Her self-discovery joins her to all other Henleyan characters who experience such discoveries, but she is different in that she is the only one experiencing the epiphany who does not also share a magical moment. She therefore is not paired with anyone at play's end, although she is not the only Henleyan character not paired. Meg Magrath and Carnelle, who do experience self-discoveries and magical moments, are not paired either.

Collard warrants a closer look because her rebelliousness is the most extreme of Henley's intentionally marginalized characters. She has slept with priests and has had an abortion. Instead of coming to Marshael's home as soon as she learned of Jamey's death, she drove to "Memphis for a wild party" (96), where her suitcase with her clothes was stolen, so she arrives at the wake wearing a muddy evening gown and men's cowboy boots. She is comfortable in these clothes, though, for they express her self-image as an individual, just as she is comfortable wearing her brother's shirt and jeans. Yet she does not want to be ostracized. Her predicament is that to go to the church service she has to dress according to cultural norms, which means borrowing an "*ill-fitted dress with ridiculous shoes and a funny-looking hat. The outfit should be the exact opposite of the image Collard likes to present of herself*" (135). The outfit is so ill fitting that she decides not to go.

This image is the second of three portraits of Collard that emerge from the drama. It is the socially conditioned image that Chick in *Crimes of the Heart,* Elain with her husband and children in *The Miss Firecracker Contest,* and Katty in *The Wake of Jamey Foster* present—and a false image for Collard. Her first image is the one that persists throughout most of the play's action. It is the image of an outsider, a nonconformist, a misfit that the naturalistic perception forms and that Collard in her self-deprecation endorses. Yet it too becomes false as the action unfolds because she is capable of change. When Marshael asks her to take the children to the service in the borrowed convertible she is driving, she accepts. Accepting responsibility, she accepts a new image as a person responsible for herself: the third image. She discovers her true self buried beneath the two false selves, but without sacrificing her individuality. Unable to get the veil she must wear over her hat, "*with a new sense of command*" she puts the veil on her head and "*then triumphantly*" puts the hat on over the veil (139). She will meet the standard for attendance at the service because she wants to participate in life, but she will meet it her way.

The two remaining plays of the 1980s offer more variations in self-discoveries, magical moments, and pairings, as well as more evidence of Henley's artistry. *The Debutante Ball* has five women, four of whom form two pairs. The fifth, who contributes to one of the four's self-discovery, is a rare character in that she experienced her epiphany before the play opens. Violet is the only domestic willing to work for the family in whose mansion the play is set on the day of the ball. To the debutante, she confides that she served time for stealing, in a fit of hatred following her mother's death, but is now "starting new."[12] To the man of the house, she confides her lifelong desire to be a circus clown, an occupation she thought denied to her until she learned that clowns are "man-made" by going to a circus school in California. "I could change myself," she sums up, "and become one, too. From then on, a whole wide life appeared up before me" (285). Her stint completed, she leaves at play's end to collect her children and belongings for the move to the West Coast.

The family's older daughter, Bliss, left when her mother was on trial for murdering her first husband, the man everyone assumed was Bliss' biological father. "To escape" (291), as she sketches in her autobiography for her stepfather's niece, she married, and, although she has a daughter by her husband, also fled him and the child when the marriage went bad. She is back home because her last boyfriend threw her belongings onto the sidewalk. With nowhere else to go, she has to plead with her mother to take her in. Her mother, Jen, does but only because she feels compelled to and only temporarily, for there is no love lost between the two. Jen was pregnant with her, by a fruit picker, when she married the first time; Bliss escaped not only because of the trial scandal but because the scandal canceled her debut; and despite protestations of affection, Jen is not pleased that she is back. In fact, the mother treats her as a servant. "Do something useful!" she orders her, prompting the older daughter to start "*polishing the silver*" (279). The woman with whom Bliss is paired is Frances, the cousin to whom she relates her life story. Frances goes to the ball with the others in her mother's "last-ditch effort to find a husband" for her (278), but since she is unattractive and deaf, she has little chance of meeting a Prince Charming. Hours later, drunk and disheveled, she wails, "'NO ONE ASKED ME TO DANCE!'" (300)

Their pairing begins with the sharing of the autobiography and climaxes in a scene following the family's wrecking the ball and a vicious argument between mother and daughter provoked by Bliss' questioning Jen as to why she favors the younger daughter, Teddy, over her. Erupting, Jen orders her, a "worthless mis-creation," to get "Out! Out! Out!" (302). Before she leaves, though, Bliss apologizes to Frances for an earlier insult, which she attributes to a deprivation she suffers. When her cousin agrees with her, the two discover themselves and each other. They are on the floor embracing, their clothes awry, when Jen enters and, seeing the compromising position, pronounces judgment on her older daughter: "You're cheap, cheap, cheap." But no longer dependent on her mother's perception for her sense of self-worth, Bliss dismisses the judgment: "I don't believe you anymore. It's not true" (306). Thrilled that her cousin likes her, Frances invites Bliss to come home with her, a situation perfect for both. Each has someone to bolster her burgeoning self-confidence, and the one has a place to live while the other has a companion to help her comfort her dying mother. Together they can form a relationship that satisfies their needs.

Just as the characters are paired, so are the images—but antithetically, a technique Henley initiated with her first plays. The lights in *Am I Blue* come up on John Polk alone in the bar, with Ashbe cautiously approaching him, and come down on the two teenagers dancing together. In the opening scene of *Crimes of the Heart,* Lenny, alone in the kitchen, is trying to make a birthday cake by sticking a candle in a cookie; in the closing scene the three sisters celebrate her birthday with a cake Meg and Babe ordered from the bakery. The image Bliss uses to describe her deprivation is a "hole," a "desperate longing" for "love" to fill her emptiness, a longing that Frances understands: "'YES. LOVE. HOLE.'" No one danced with the cousin at the ball, but Bliss does, for the "*moment is very potent*" (306). They do not discover an infusion from without the self, although in Henley's imaginative world a character's extending herself or himself to another helps to awaken feelings in the recipient, but a welling up of feelings within the self that the culture has denied or driven underground.

This scene combines the two experiences that Henley heretofore developed separately though relatedly: the self-discovery and the magical moment. Marshael's and Brocker's discoveries may occur at the same time, but the two characters are not together, and Collard, who has her epiphany the following morning, is not present at their magical moment. Bliss and Frances, however, simultaneously discover themselves and each other, and their discovery is the magical moment. Furthermore, the combined experience incarnates an indefiniteness in *The Wake of Jamey Foster.* Marshael describes the effect of Jamey's abandonment as a "hole" (119) shot through her. When she runs from the house, she is searching for "something" (134) to fill the hole. In order for her to offer Brocker a second chance, the search had to be successful, but the "something" is not named. The spectator infers love and forgiveness from the pair's interaction in the closing scene. The scene in *The Debutante Ball* names "'LOVE'" as that which will fulfill and dramatizes it as the pair embrace, uniting the two, with Bliss feeling the "*fullness*" (306) of Frances' breasts, a fullness that is antithetical to the emptiness both feel prior to the scene. The antithetical images continue through their departure. Bliss is dependent upon her mother for a place to live. Since Jen forgot to meet Frances at the station, the police had to search for her. After Frances invites Bliss to come to her home, the two women enter the parlor together, preparatory to departing the mansion, "*carrying Bliss' luggage*" (312).

Women can cause one another's low self-esteem. When Jen tells her husband that they must abort their younger daughter's pregnancy, she says that Teddy's life cannot be "ruined" (304) as hers was. She is referring to being pregnant with Bliss by a fruit picker as the reason she married, an act that eventually led to her first husband's death and the family scandal. That she blames Bliss is clear from her calling her older daughter a "worthless mis-creation" (302). Yet in an androcentric culture, men are the principal detractors from a woman's worth. As Collard relates her autobiography in *The Wake of Jamey Foster,* she was the father's favorite whom he wanted to be a lawyer until she scored below average on an intelligence test. "Oh, God!" she wails. "I was nothing in his eyes from then on! Just dumb and stupid and nothing!" (127).

Women can impose their wills on others. When Teddy tries to excuse herself from the ball, Jen cannot grant her request: "I've tried so hard to make this night just what you wanted" (283). The truth is that she is using her daughter to get revenge on the town that ostracized her following the murder. Yet men are Henley's more domineering characters even when they are absent. *Am I Blue*'s John Polk goes to college because his father believes he "should go to business school" to become "management-minded" (77) so that he can help run the family's soybean farm. The Magrath sisters of *Crimes of the Heart* live lives their Old Granddaddy planned for them. Lenny's defense of him is that "all he ever wanted was the best for us." Meg agrees, but with reservations: "Well, I guess it was; but sometimes I wonder what we wanted" (37). When present, the men can be like Wayne, asserting dominance by trying to change Collard's name and referring to Katty as a "twat" (114).

Men can help women discover themselves, as Doc helps Meg. Yet more often than not in the plays of the 1980s, women help one another, as Marshael helps Collard by asking her to let the children ride in her car to the church. Meg and Babe, Bliss and Frances, and Teddy and Jen and Violet are other examples. Jen and Teddy are paired in the opening scene in which the mother is coaching the younger daughter on her entrance that evening at the ball, an event that will reinstate the family in

Hattiesburg's good graces. But it is immediately apparent that something is wrong with the daughter, who disfigures herself at every opportunity. The instance that gets everyone's attention occurs in the closing moments of act 1, when she starts to pull apart her hairpiece to rid it of imagined rats after the grandmother, remarking on her resemblance to her late father, told her she could "see" the blood of the father's side of the family "inside" her (293). What Teddy wants to expel is the something festering inside her, and it is not rats. As act 1 ends, the something is the fetus she is carrying, the result of having given herself to a mutilated man whom she humiliated, yet as act 2 unfolds, the something is guilt for having killed her father while trying to protect her mother from him. She committed the ultimate transgression against the male authority that reduces a woman to nothing and that would have either killed or disfigured Jen had she not acted first.

As the passing years of the 1980s move deeper into the decade, so do Henley's characters bury their true selves beneath deeper layers. Babe has buried her true self beneath an unhappy marriage, a crime, and a fear of inherited mental instability, but she never conceals her role in the shooting of Zackery, and by the end of act 1 she reveals the truth about the marriage and the shooting, thereby preparing the surface for the buried self's release: her discovery, in act 3, that she is neither crazy nor alone. With the layering of selves comes a stratifying of perception of the selves. Carnelle's cousins do not think she can win the contest, but they support her, and Delmount plans to split with her the proceeds from the sale of the house. In *The Debutante Ball* the naturalistic perception comes from within the family. Bliss and Frances have buried their true selves beneath the family's perception of them, and their perception of themselves, as losers.

Teddy suffers not because Jen perceives her the way she perceives Bliss but because Jen wants her to go to the ball, an event that necessitates the daughter's putting on a false self, with its false face, to conceal the self that killed her father—a self that in her guilt she feels is apparent to others, particularly when they make suggestive statements. For example, during an angry exchange between stepfather Hank and cousin Brighton about Jen's getting away with murder, the latter tells the former to "ask Teddy. She knows the truth." Teddy rushes to the bathroom to put on "*massive amounts of makeup*" (290). The strategy of concealment does not work, however, because Teddy's guilt-stricken self that killed her father impinges on the mask until she confesses. Once she confesses, her true self, the self beneath the killer, can emerge.

Beneath the faces that Henleyan characters don to meet the world there is no realm of edenic innocence. Bliss is a good example: she left her husband and daughter when the marriage failed and has made little effort to communicate with her child since then. When she tries to return to them, only because she needs a place to live, and is rebuffed by her ex-husband, she laughs, "Oh, well, maybe it was a mistake sleeping with every one of his friends before leaving the state" (305). Another possible confusion must also be clarified. Certain Henleyan images such as the mirror appear in multiple plays and take on greater significance as the playwright develops as an artist. The "hole" that Marshael refers to and that becomes the basis of simultaneous self-discoveries and magical moment in *The Debutante Ball* is one such symbol, and this study will continue to examine the artist's obsessive images. But every repetition is not symbolic. Some repetitions are nothing more than ideas repeated in varying language. In her rage at losing the contest, Carnelle turns on

Mac Sam, who makes her "*sick*" for being "*sick*" (197). Collard's whining about being stupid exasperates Marshael: "I'm so sick of that excuse I could retch up blood!" (121). This image is a mere repetition and not a development.

What does develop, in addition to obsessive imagery, is the Henleyan conflict. The most fundamental conflict is between society's naturalistic perception of the outsider and the outsider's striving to overcome such a perception by recovering or releasing the self beneath the self that is imposed by the perception and accepted by the character's self-deprecation. In *The Debutante Ball,* the conflict is between concealing the true self under the false face that participation in life requires and revealing the true self because of guilt. Teddy's alternately piling on makeup and slashing her face prepares the surface for the release of the buried self as killer. But the killer is also a false self; it is not who Teddy really is. To recover her true self beneath this false self means confessing to the killing, with the risk of proving the cultural perception correct: the false self and the true self are one and the same. She must confess, however, in order to heal. No matter what they have done or been, so that they might recover the self that is capable of loving and being loved, Henley's characters must journey through the selves their divided psyches have spawned. Only then can they heal—and be whole.

Teddy and Jen are paired in the play's closing scene, but now the roles are reversed, with the mother in the bathtub and the daughter beside it applying ointment to her mother's outbreak of psoriasis. The skin disorder is an interesting image because it is the image Teddy uses in the closing scene of act 1 to characterize her spiritual condition as it manifests itself in the body she keeps trying to disfigure: "Oh, Mama, it just won't ever heal up. It's raw scabs over raw scabs and now it's all ripping away"

(294). Of course, confessing her guilt does heal her. Jen does not heal presumably because she will not journey through her masks to the truth of herself, a truth that lies buried beneath her courtroom testimony that she "acted in self-defense" (299), noble though the testimony was in shielding her daughter from a murder charge. She certainly knows herself. To Hank she says that "there's just some blackness buried so deep inside my chest you never could have pulled it out with a pair of pliers" (313).

Interaction with Violet, the maid, enables Teddy to bring out the blackness buried inside her chest. When in act 2 Violet stops her from slashing her face, Teddy tells the maid how she got pregnant and why she gave herself to the mutilated man: "I was at a point, you see, where I couldn't take any more, ah, bad feelings, guilt. Just no more." Violet's admission that to get "things" off her chest, she "used to write secrets in jars and bury the jars outside in the dirt" prompts Teddy's admission that she too has "hidden things" on her chest: "Certain acts. Irredeemable acts" (298). Later when the daughter likens the feelings in her chest to flashes of lightning but without the thunder that would release and relieve the feelings, the maid gives her the final piece of advice: "Then you make it thunder" (307). She does. She confesses to striking the blow that killed her father.

Violet contributes another image indicating the change that accompanies self-discovery. Early in the play, she claims that a bird is a "sign a' change" (270). After repeating, in detail, her confession to stepfather Hank, the lawyer who got Jen acquitted at the trial, Teddy glances at the balcony and calls to the maid to look, for there by the white branch is a bird. That the mother immediately enters "*trembling like a newborn bird*" (314) would seem to contradict her condition as imaged in the psoriasis, but Jen is an ambiguous figure: a mother who arranges one daughter's life while distancing herself from the other daughter and a woman whose relationship with her husband spirals downward from an act-1 pledge of mutual love to an act-2 separation until their final moments together. When he says that he will miss her, she replies in such a way as to suggest that she prefers he not leave. Perhaps the explanation for Jen is in her motivation. Both she and Carnelle see in a social event the vehicle for claiming a place in society, but whereas Carnelle's motivation is a desire to win respect, Jen's is a desire to get revenge on "everyone in this town who ever shunned or ostracized" (276) the family following the scandal. Her desire can so fill her soul that she does not feel the emptiness that her daughters and Frances feel.

No such ambiguity surrounds Teddy in the play's closing moments. From her cousin Brighton, she secures permission to stay at his lake cottage until she is on her feet. Then attending her mother, she delivers her speech of self-discovery. She can "smell the rain coming and . . . feel it's gonna start to thunder." As she pictures herself standing in the rain and thunder, she concludes: "And these arms will want to hold onto somebody and have their arms holding onto me" (315). Having expelled the blackness buried within her, she can develop an interiority filled with the need to love and be loved.

Before acknowledging her role in her father's death, Teddy tells Violet that she "can't start new" because she has "too many things" on her chest and although she keeps "trying to push them down," they keep "gripping back up" at her (307). Just as southern culture tries to repress its second-class citizens but they keep resisting, so do these outsiders keep trying to repress their secrets, but the inner life, the interiority, keeps pushing outward, even in Jen. In a 1999 interview, Henley contrasted Teddy and

Jen at play's end. Unlike the daughter, who experiences a "renewal," the mother's "literal body is decaying as much as her secrets have decayed her insides, because her insides are becoming harder to mask. Everything that has been internalized and hidden is now coming through."[13]

The naturalistic plays, however, do not dramatize the journey that must be taken to the interior. For critic Jonnie Guerra, having the change in a heroine's development take place offstage is a weakness in the portrayal of her quest. Henley's plays attempt to portray the female quest for autonomy, but the playwright's reliance on traditionally patriarchal "form and dramaturgy undermine to some degree her thematic intention." A few pages later, Guerra writes, "Another weakness in Henley's portrayal of female quest is suggested by her habit of interrupting its presentation on stage: some heroines reach a crucial point in their development by going offstage and then coming back to announce the change that has occurred. . . . Henley's dilemma, of course, is to represent on stage situations of self-contemplation and insight, events that happen in mental space."[14] A stage image for the event in mental space, or interiority, does not appear until the 1990s, although the last written play of the 1980s, *The Lucky Spot,*[15] is both the culmination of the naturalistic decade and a transition to the innovative decade.

Act 1 of *The Lucky Spot* is presented naturalistically in that the setting is a farmhouse in rural Louisiana that Reed Hooker won in a card game and converted into a dance hall. With him are three others, recognizably Henleyan. The male employee, "plagued by self-doubt,"[16] is Turnip, whom a "lot of people think of . . . as stupid" (241). The female employee is Cassidy, a fifteen-year-old whom Hooker won in a card game and has impregnated; her previous owner, from whom Hooker won her, called her a "godless bag a' stench," fed her "cow feed," and "branded" her (244–45). Although she knows that Hooker does not love her, she expects him to marry her to prevent the child from being a bastard. The lone taxi dancer, Lacey, has never had much luck with men. The one who was supposed to marry her jilted her; the last one she was with "tried t' drowned" her "in the bathtub" (224).

Into the dance hall comes Sue Jack, Hooker's wife and former taxi dancer who has just been released from prison, where she served time for throwing over a balcony railing a woman she caught in bed with her husband. She returns to him because she loves him and believes he wants her back. When, however, she realizes that not only did he not send for her but that he intends to divorce her and marry Cassidy, she takes the shotgun and shoots up the room. That act provokes a brawl, for despite her argument that she has changed, Hooker sees no true self struggling to emerge from beneath a false self; she is the self she always was: a "stupid slut" (234). When, however, he realizes that he loves her and wants her back, the situation reverses. To convince him that she is not worthy of him, she reveals a self she has kept concealed.

The motif of the neglected or rejected child runs throughout Henley's plays. Her parents divorced, *Am I Blue*'s Ashbe lives in a "*pig sty*" (74) of an apartment with her father, who is frequently out of town and, spectators learn from a phone conversation she has with him, unable to control his drinking habit. In *Crimes of the Heart*, the Magrath sisters' recollection of the funeral of their mother, who committed suicide after their father abandoned the family, is "crying the whole morning long" (38). As Carnelle relates her autobiography to Popeye in *The Miss Firecracker Contest*, her mother died when she was "barely a year old." Her father raised her until he "couldn't stand" her "any longer," at which time he "dropped" her "off to live with" her cousins' family (152). Yet an interesting shift occurs in this play; the perspective changes to that of the mother. When Elain arrives in Brookhaven, having left her husband and two little boys, her attitude is cavalier: "Oh, children manage in this world. Don't ask me about them" (159). In other plays, Collard had an abortion, Bliss left her child with her ex-husband, and Teddy has a miscarriage. The experience touched Collard and scars Teddy, but although the debutante miscarries immediately following her revelation of the killing, the rejected child motif and the secret involving culpability are not linked until *The Lucky Spot.* In each of the motif's three instances, the secret is withheld longer. Babe reveals the reason she shot Zackery at the end of act 1; Teddy reveals the killing of her father at the end of act 2's first scene; and Sue Jack reveals the negligence that resulted in her son's death at the end of act 2's second scene. Each instance reveals a greater culpability, from wounding an abusive husband to killing an abusive father and husband to abrogating responsibility for a child. Since each instance indicates a greater culpability, each secret has to be summoned from a greater depth within the heroine.

To plumb this depth, *The Lucky Spot* links the summoning with two of Henley's repeated images: the mirror that contributes to Collard's self-discovery and the hole that contributes to Marshael's self-discovery. When Sue Jack arrives at the Lucky Spot, she sees a mirror in her friends' faces, but the image, confirmed by the hand mirror, is not one she wants to be reminded of for two reasons. Knowing her face shows the ravages of three years in prison, she wants to look attractive for Hooker. But she also wants him to see past the exterior self to a change that has taken place within her: "I'm not the same as I was, Reed. Go on and look at me. You see, I'm not the same." As she talks, she tells him about the only belonging she had in prison: a photo of herself taken just before she left home years earlier. "I used to take out that picture and look at it. I kept on pondering over it. I swear it confused me so much, wondering where she was—that girl in the picture. I could not imagine where she'd departed to—so unknowingly, so unexpectedly" (231).

The photo is another mirror, but one that reverses the relationship between the subject and the image that appears only when the subject looks into the mirror. In this surreal tale, since the mirror retains the image of a subject-self who has departed, it does not give a new image when Sue Jack looks into it. No longer the girl she was when she left home or the woman she was when living with Hooker, she does not know who she is. Although Sue Jack does not use the metaphor that Marshael, Bliss, and Frances use, she feels a hole, an emptiness, in her being because no mirror gives her an image of her interiority, where the change has taken place. She accepts the identity her friends' faces and the hand mirror give her, but that image is of the exterior self: her body. She wants confirmation of the new interior self; she needs to love and be loved, for love emanates from the interior life. She therefore goes berserk when she learns that Hooker plans to divorce her and marry Cassidy. His naturalistic perception of her does what the dominant culture has always done: deny her interiority, her spiritual nature. And in so doing, he denies not only the change in herself she feels but the love she feels for him, the one reality that enabled her to endure the assaults on her body and soul while in prison, the one reality that can fill the hole in her being. "The one thing I know as sure as the smell of spring rain," she screams at Cassidy, "is that

I utterly, hopelessly love that rotten, worthless son of a bitch!" (233) Grabbing the shotgun, she shoots up the room.

When Sue Jack next enters the dance hall, in act 2, she is wearing a "*glamorous tight-fitted dress from her past*" (238). Believing that the love between her and Hooker is blasted, she reverts to who she was before the prison term, and finding neither an outlet for nor confirmation of her interior change, she reverts to identifying herself through an exterior change. Like other Henleyan heroines, she returns to a past relationship in the process of self-discovery. The return interweaves the four strands of Henley's art under examination. Learning that Hooker still loves her, she resolves to disabuse him of any hope he has of reconciliation by revealing the secret of her negligence as instrumental in their son's death. Emptied of any hope herself, she challenges to a game of cards Hooker's adversary, a man named Carmichael who has a claim to the dance hall property. She knows he will take the challenge because he is the brother of the woman she hospitalized and he makes his desire for her obvious. Losing, she starts to leave with Carmichael to pay off the wager, her body against his claim, but Hooker intervenes. Surrendering his claim to the property as payment of her wager, he spares her another assault on the sanctity of her person, for he has come to recognize that he loves her, that each has an interiority to be shared with the other.

Hooker's embrace actualizes the two remaining images in the interweaving strands. As he holds her tightly, Sue Jack "*stares at him dumbstruck,*" seeing in his face a mirror giving back the image she sought to fill the vacuum left by the departing girl in the photo, the image of a woman worthy of being loved, and "*tears stream down her face*" (257) in an overflow of emotion surging within her. Plumbing the past has paradoxically freed her, as it frees other Henleyan questers, for a new future. The following morning she enters the Lucky Spot from "walking. And thinking" about how she misses Hooker. "A lot. A real lot" (261–62), she tells him. Now love, renewed, can flourish. Although admitting that she does not "know how to be" because of all the "muddy goddamn water" (262) in her past, she discovers nonetheless that she can be. With the hog stolen and the group facing a Christmas without dinner, she volunteers to make a pumpkin dinner, a "treat" (262) she and Hooker have not had in years. Reconciled with the man she loves, Sue Jack is reconciled with herself.

This study has referred to a character's selves as true and false, but a self should not be thought of as existing solely within a character until it is replaced by another self. That characters have multiple and not unitary selves *The Lucky Spot* illustrates, as it does Henley's technique of developing images with minute variations until they become symbolic and the scenes built on them become charged. When Sue Jack first arrives, her hair "all cropped off" (225), she is in her present, subdued self hoping that Hooker accepts her as changed from the self she was when they were together, that her drinking, brawling, gambling self is no longer her true self. When he rejects her, however, she begins drinking, brawling, and gambling with Carmichael. No longer subdued, the past self is the present self; she is the self she was when they were together, as symbolized by the "*glamorous tight-fitted dress from her past*" (238). Yet at least two other selves exist beneath the dress, struggling to make their presence known. She has "*restyled her hair*" (238) and after gathering her belongings wears a "*black hat with berries*" (241). The restyling suggests that despite the tough exterior, there is a sensitivity, a vulnerability, yearning for something redemptive in life that would open new possibilities, and the decorated hat recalls the neglected child in herself, the child that would love to regain something of the innocence lost when the girl in the photo wearing a "straw hat decorated with violets" (231) departed.

Sue Jack's final entrance reconciles all the selves in her. She wears the same dress from the past, but the stage directions do not have to emphasize its glamour or its tight fit. The dress fits because the past is hers, a past she accepted when she revealed her secret. Not wearing a hat decorated with berries, she "*carries a branch of holly*" (259), as traditional as the mistletoe that Turnip brings on Christmas Day, the time of the play's final scene. On a day for celebrating the entrance of new life into an old world, she has recovered that which was lost. As reunited husband and wife "*kiss passionately*" (262), they renew their love for each other, and renewing love, they open the possibility of a new future.

Reconciled with the partner from whom she was estranged, Sue Jack is reconciled with herself: the conflict, like the imagery, develops as Henley's artistry develops. Once a character accepts the self-deprecation that follows from other characters' naturalistic perceptions, the character begins to fracture into different selves, all of which coexist, although at different times and for different reasons some dominate and some are in abeyance. These selves have been called true and false selves, but perhaps selves with differing claims and allegiances are better descriptors. Lenny Magrath is divided between her need for love and her shame at being unable to meet the cultural claim that women have children; she is divided between her need for love and her allegiance to Old Granddaddy, who she feels has a legitimate claim to her caregiving skills. Teddy is divided between her guilt and her allegiance to Jen, who is herself divided between her allegiance to her daughter and her desire for revenge. Abandoned by the death of her mother and the desertion of her father, Cassidy is divided between the knowledge that Hooker does not love her and the need to have a father for her child, her primary allegiance whose claim supersedes all other claims. The persistence of past selves, whether lurking in mirrors or photos, in narratives or dreams, reveals the depth of the claims they make on the characters. Sue Jack's card game forces a confrontation between Hooker and Carmichael over their claims. The outcome forces her to go walking and thinking about the divisions within herself.

Fracturing is not confined to the self, and characters are not the only forces making claims on the self. Cultural forms and conventions make claims as well. In the opening moments of *The Debutante Ball,* Teddy asks Bliss whether men know the difference between the makeup a woman applies and the face beneath the makeup. Her sister replies that they are "aware it's something of an illusion." Then why, Teddy asks, "do they want it? It's all a big trick" (273). Fortunately for Bliss, who has no answer, the ringing of the doorbell allows her to change the subject.

Act 2 of *The Lucky Spot* is a universe different from that of act 1 and the preceding naturalistic dramas. As Turnip questions, life is the big trick: "What does any of it matter?! All these miserable people butting around. Trying so hard. For what?! Before it's all over every one of 'em's gonna be stone cold dead! Absolutely every one of 'em. (*Snapping his fingers.*) Dead! Dead! Dead! So what the hell are they all sweating?!" (240). Neither is he alone in recognizing that all forms and conventions, all activity and effort have been shattered into fragments. For Sue Jack, the "whole world's a joke" (246). In this recognition, life's surface is deceptive because it conceals existence without love, existence disappearing in the jaws of annihilating death. With existence devoid of a purpose in a "godless" (212, 233, 244) world cut adrift from its traditional mooring, life is absurd.

Life does not become absurd in *The Lucky* Spot—it has always been so in Henley's imaginative world, as attested to by critics' use of such words describing this world as chaotic, meaningless, fragmented, sterile, and, of course, absurd. William W. Demastes's study dates from the decade's end. Acknowledging the insight of Stanley Kauffmann, who reviewed *Crimes of the Heart* early in the 1980s, Demastes writes that "Henley's play presents, as Kauffmann argues, 'the tension between the fierce lurking lunacy underlying the small-town life she knows so well and the sunny surface that tries to accommodate it' ('Two Cheers' 55). As such, her work escapes the intellectual detachment of the French absurdists and existentialists, and because it takes the horrors of life out of the lecture halls and puts them in a kitchen, it argues that the absurd has an immediacy and relevance to daily existence that other works can't claim to argue."[17]

In theater of the absurd, absurdity is the imposition of a surface order onto a subsurface disorder: the rationality of language and logic, for example, onto the irrationality of existential experience. Absurdity in Henley's theater is the imposition of culturally prescribed forms of behavior and expression onto needs and aspirations or the sanctioned life's denial or repression of the renegade life. Even nonconformists contribute to the absurdity. Hooker does so by attempting to realize his dream of a dance hall in the converted farmhouse that he will not sell to Carmichael despite the latter's offer of a fair price for the property. He imposes "rules" (250) onto the first of the second act's two dance sequences, with the result that the people within the hall are disconnected one from another in anything but a superficial way. The lone patron must rent a necktie and purchase a ticket, which he must hand to the partner of his choice, before he may dance. Employees may not dance with each other unless they purchase a ticket. One of them must ring a bell signaling the end of the dance so that the patron must use another ticket if he wants to continue dancing.

Yet to use Teddy's idiom in *The Debutante Ball*, the repressed life keeps "gripping back up," with the result that within the naturalistic plays, both characters and their audiences recognize not only the incompatibility of the surface and subsurface but also their interaction. Janet L. Gupton's analysis of *Crimes of the Heart* and *The Debutante Ball* gives a new descriptive adjective for the subsurface. The Magrath sisters, Teddy, and Bliss are "'unruly women'" whose rebellion against the traditional roles for southern women challenges the foundations of southern patriarchal society.[18] With the introduction of this new descriptive adjective—"ruled"—the critic can now see the divided self in Henley's drama and the drama itself as the tension-conflict-interplay between a ruled surface and an unruly subsurface, with characters before they discover themselves yielding to one or the other pressure in the antinomy.

By act 2 of *The Lucky Spot*, the pressures imposed by a ruled surface and erupting in an unruly subsurface are so intense that Sue Jack surrenders to life's lack of purpose. For Carmichael, Hooker's dream of establishing a dance hall in rural Louisiana during the Great Depression is just that: a dream with a "Chinaman's chance" (216) of success. To ensure its failure, he rounds up locals to whom Hooker owes money to loot the property. Knowing she cannot stay, Sue Jack learns that no one outside the

Lucky Spot will take her in; one friend she felt sure she could count on "stopped in an alleyway t' pick up some change and got hit by a falling flower box" (239). Realizing it is time to "pay off . . . debts, stand up, and leave the goddamn table" (246), she challenges Carmichael to a card game. When her husband intervenes to spare her giving her body as payment, her response is "Look, this is nothing to me. He's just one guy, one night" (257).

Yet of the plays of the 1980s, *The Lucky Spot* has the greatest recognition of love's power. The play's subject is love. It opens with a conversation in which Turnip, learning from Cassidy that Hooker plans to marry her, asks her whether she believes he loves her, a question repeated not long afterwards by Lacey, the taxi dancer. Talking about the past love of Hooker and Sue Jack for each other and the effect of their son's death on that love, the dance hall employees reveal their attitudes toward love—Turnip wondering whether he will ever have a girlfriend—and their experiences with it—Lacey's blighted romances. No scene ever goes very long without the word being spoken. When, for example, Hooker realizes that he loves Sue Jack after fighting with her and ordering her to leave after Christmas Day, Turnip comments, "I swear, I pray I never fall in love. It seems like such a terrible thing" (253). Yet the closing scene hints at a pairing between Turnip and Lacey. Cassidy's experience is more than just hinted at; she shouts out her discovery that "maybe love ain't a made-up lie like Santa Claus or something" (259). Discovering love's power is her self-discovery: "Why, this could be the beginning of my future" (262). In contrast, in *The Miss Firecracker Contest,* Carnelle throws her arms around Mac Sam when he tells her how much the times they were together mean to him but declines his offer to spend the night together, and Elain returns to her husband but not because she loves him or her children. Sue Jack and Hooker are the naturalistic plays' ultimate couple, transmitting an "*electric passion*" between them (257) and kissing "*passionately*" (262).

The interaction and interpenetration of a purposeless universe and love's power counter the absurdity that pervades Henley's theater. Reversals abound. At play's opening, Sue Jack and Hooker are alienated from themselves and each other, but by play's end they have discovered their true feelings and are reconciled, reversing the decade's beginning, in which Babe shoots Zackery. Beginning with Ashbe's statement to John Polk that "Daddy's out of town and Mama lives in Atlanta" (73), Henley's plays pillory marriage as a form in conflict with its contents, a surface that remains legally binding only if the submissive, like Elain's husband and Katty, allow the unruly, like Elain and Wayne, to dishonor its rules. Renewing their love, Sue Jack and Hooker revitalize marriage not as a cultural form but as a living bond with which they curb their unruly natures for the sake of a union, grounded in love, that they can shape as they grow. Writing about love's value in characters supporting one another in Henley's early plays, Nancy Hargrove finds "family love providing this support more often than romantic love."[19] By decade's end both kinds of love provide this support, and family love is not restricted to sisters. Love has been developing from giving a sense of self-worth to the isolated self to connecting two isolated selves to actualizing a community. In the first of act 2's dance sequences in *The Lucky Spot,* Cassidy declines Turnip's invitation to dance, and Carmichael declines Lacey's invitation. The second sequence, a magical moment, is communal and celebratory; the family is humankind. "*Men dance with women, men dance with men, women dance with women. People dance alone. Everyone dances with everyone else as the lights slowly fade to blackout and the music continues to play*" (263). The image is that of fragmented life made whole by love, for in Henley's plays of the 1980s, love gives meaning to an otherwise absurd existence.

The increasing of love's power, culminating in *The Lucky Spot,* makes the spectator aware of the incompatibility between the culture's surface, the naturalistic perception that either denies an interior life to the outsider or perceives it as a welter of uncontrollable animal urges, and the outsider's subsurface, the interior spiritual life from which love emanates. *The Lucky Spot* is also a transitional play to Henley's experimental decade because three shifts in emphasis, increasing in the naturalistic decade and culminating in *The Lucky Spot,* make the spectator aware of the incompatibility between a drama's naturalistic surface and its symbolic subsurface. The first shift is away from the body's exterior. *The Miss Firecracker Contest* contains the greatest emphasis on the significance of clothing in defining the self. When Elain arrives in Brookhaven, Carnelle is disappointed that she did not bring the dress she asked her to, the red antebellum dress the cousin wore at the Natchez Pilgrimage the year she was married, because it is "perfect" for Carnelle's "thematic color" (157) in the contest. Elain tells her to wait until she passes the audition and is one of the five selected to compete for the title. When Carnelle is selected, Elain sends for the dress, but since it arrives the day before the contest and does not fit right, Carnelle is apprehensive about the beauty pageant segment. She should be, for she trips on the skirt and falls, provoking laughter from the audience, and the hooligans in the crowd who know her as Miss Hot Tamale heckle her. She is trapped in her old self because she tried to create a new self by imitating her cousin. She does not discover herself until the final scene, a recognition that does not involve clothing.

Each subsequent play continues to de-emphasize clothing's significance in the heroine's self-image. Marshael is in a black dress throughout *The Wake of Jamey Foster* until the final scene; wearing a slip, she wraps a blanket around herself before going out on the balcony. In the same scene, Collard takes command of the culturally sanctioned clothes by putting her hat on over the veil she must wear in church. To say that Teddy is unhappy with her self-image is an understatement. Neither is she impressed with her wardrobe. She gives her fur stole to Frances to wear to the ball, and she ruins her gown at the event. Not until the final scene, dressed in jeans and shirt, is she the image of inner peace, a young woman who no longer feels "like it's never gonna get better" (315). At one point in the play, first Bliss and then Frances reach under their skirts, remove their panties, and throw them over the balcony to the ground below. Sue Jack wears two outfits: a "*hand-me-down dress, a thin wool coat, and flat ugly shoes*" (224) in act 1 and a glamorous dress from her past in act 2. The second outfit is a reversion to an earlier self that the self-discovery absorbs.

A second shift is the increasing emphasis on the interior self. All of Henley's questers strive to discover themselves, but Sue Jack's striving is the most intense. She was removed from society for three years, tells of her disorientation looking at the photo, is homeless, and admits she does not know who she is. "'cause even when I don't know who in this godless world I am, or was, or ever will be" (233), she says to Cassidy, she knows she loves Hooker. Yet he rejects her; she is rejected at her homecoming. Separated from the world, Sue Jack is separated from the self the world—her culture and family—determined for her. Losing the self she should be, she has to find a self she can be, but she cannot do so until she returns to the past to descend into her interior self, releasing her repressed guilt in her confession and her repressed feelings for Hooker in her renewed love.

The third shift in emphasis is in Henley's mode of production. Excluding the statement or statements indicating where the play takes place—in a particular town or house—*The Wake of Jamey Foster* contains the most elaborate stage directions for a play's setting. Sixteen sentences name twenty-four items of decor, some of them plural: furniture, rugs, books, wreaths, and so on. If rooms, doors, window, balcony, and tree are added to this list, the items total thirty-four. Each of the two succeeding plays of the 1980s de-emphasizes the naturalistic setting. To describe its setting, *The Debutante Ball* has ten sentences with eleven items, two of them plural: floors and faucets. *The Lucky Spot* has five sentences with eleven items, two of them plural: tables and chairs. The first play of the 1990s, *Abundance,* devotes only one sentence with no details to the setting, and succeeding plays similarly specify non-naturalistic settings.

The act that spells the end of naturalism's reign as a mode of production occurs toward the end of act 1 of *The Lucky Spot* when Sue Jack, realizing that Hooker did not send for her and does not want her, grabs the shotgun and shoots up the room including the jukebox. In the introduction to the play, Henley explains how the act solved a technical problem. Music by black artists best captured the mood of the 1930s, the time of the play, but she knew that "this music would never be on a 1930s jukebox." Sue Jack's shooting the jukebox "to smithereens" (xv) forces Hooker, who has to have music for the dance hall, to play the previous owner's "old race records" (247) stored in the attic.

The act shatters much more than a stage prop, for it shatters the culturally sanctioned music to release underground music, music not in jukeboxes because it was not accepted by the dominant culture.

Shattering the containing surface, the shooting releases the repressed subsurface. In only two plays of the 1980s, a character who impacts significantly on the action does not appear until act 2. Their names are similar, Mac Sam and Sam, as is each one's function in the play in which he appears. Mac Sam in *The Miss Firecracker Contest* subverts cultural expectations for a man by earning his living selling balloons. He is also subversive in refusing to die despite having been "almost choked to death" by his "umbilical cord at birth" (178) and suffering from numerous ailments. Not an allegorical figure, he is not completely naturalistic either. A contradiction as evidenced by in the initial description of him—"*in drastically poor health*" yet "*extraordinarily sensual,*" with eyes that "*manage to be magnetic and bloodshot at the same time*" (175)—he embodies that which defies explanation; he embodies the irrational. And he is the catalyst for Carnelle's self-discovery by directing her attention to the irrational.[20]

The second such character appears in *The Lucky Spot.* With Sue Jack and Hooker vowing to part after Christmas and the evening a "dream so shattered" that Hooker "can't even remember what the pieces were" (246), a lone patron enters the dance hall who boosts everyone's spirits. Because he has dedicated his life to caring for a wife "blind all her life," Sam overturns the cultural tradition in which women subordinate their desires to those of their brothers, fathers, and husbands or, as Karen L. Laughlin demonstrates in her study of *Crimes of the Heart,* imitate the desires of Old Granddaddy.[21] To Cassidy's question about missing his deceased wife, he responds, "Oh yeah. She loved watermelon. I used t' slice it up for her and pick out all the seed" (250). Exemplifying love's devotion, he embodies emotions the dominant culture deems renegade. It is while Sam is present that Hooker realizes he "can't help" (252) loving Sue Jack, that Turnip senses love can be a "terrible thing" (253), and that Cassidy feels the "*electric passion*" (257) between the husband and wife. And he is the catalyst for Cassidy's self-discovery that she can hope to meet someone who will give her a "slice of watermelon and pick out all the seeds" (259). Releasing Hooker from his promise to marry her removes the last obstacle to his reunion with Sue Jack. Bringing sugar candies to the Christmas celebration, Sam is one of the dancers in the closing magical moment.

By ending naturalism's reign as a mode of production in her work, Henley ends the reign of theater's sanctioned—or ruled—form but a surface unable to accommodate theater's generating—or unruly—subsurface, a form against which the contemporary American theater rebels. John Guare is another playwright representative of the movement away from naturalism. In the preface to a volume of his plays, he traces the development of his theatrical imagination beginning with three plays he wrote at age eleven through his discovery that playwrights could put the unconscious on the stage crystallizing his different responses to the different plays and productions he had been seeing. "Don't show me a theater," he writes, "whose prime focus is only creating an illusion of surface reality, where the play is true because—look—it's a real room with real water running into the kitchen sink." He concludes with a realization he had in the late 1960s:

> what the playwright does with the icon of naturalism, the kitchen sink, is the story of twentieth-century playwrighting. Does the playwright elect to keep that kitchen sink to soothe the audience? Does the playwright dismantle the kitchen sink and take the audience into dangerous terrain? How the playwright resolves the tension between surface reality and inner reality, how the playwright restores the theater to its true nature as a place of poetry, song, joy, a place of darkness where the bright truth is told, that war against the kitchen sink is ultimately the history of our theater.[22]

Throughout the 1980s, Henley moves toward imaging the separation from the surface reality of the exterior world and the culturally determined self as a journey into the inner reality of the isolated, fragmented self. This journey is a "continuing existential quest for meaning, dignity, and selfhood,"[23] with love the one force reconciling the self both with itself and with others, thereby creating magical moments that render existence meaningful. The critic can gauge the difference between this decade and the one that follows by two points of comparison. The full-length play that opens the 1980s is set in a kitchen; the play that opens the 1990s is set in a dangerous terrain. In the first act of each of Henley's five full-length plays of the 1980s, a character or characters return home to a naturalistic setting. In the first act of the play that opens the 1990s, two women are on a journey away from their naturalistic home. With the change in the mode of production, a new style of writing begins to emerge through which Henley presents the interior journey. This change means that the quester discovers something in the depths of the interior that is given voice to through a new style of writing: a force equal to love and therefore a new conflict with new competing claims on the self with which the quester must contend. The boon, however, is that the character who separates from the self and the world is reunited with the self and the world on a new creative ground.

CHAPTER 3

1990s—Initial Experiments

Abundance is Henley's first play of the 1990s and the first with a locale not in Mississippi or Louisiana. A single statement sums up the setting: "Wyoming Territory and later in St. Louis, Missouri."[1] The naturalistic plays, which cover a few days at most, are typically divided into two acts, each of two or three scenes. This play, which "spans twenty-five years, starting in the late 1860s" (4), is fragmented into two acts, the first comprising eleven scenes, the second, eight scenes; a scene can be as short as a single page of text. Following one another in episodic succession, scenes take place inside a cabin where the settings Henley specifies limit the furniture to an item or two, or outside the cabin on an open landscape. Another difference between this play and those of the 1980s is the addition of a new technique for Henley: structuring the action around a gap, subsequent references to which cast doubt on what happened during the absent scene.

The text of *Abundance* has two gaps, but what happens during the second gap is not in question. Act 1 closes with the disappearance of a woman, followed in performance by an intermission. Act 2 opens five years later with her return, transformed. The woman is Bess Johnson. Her singing as she waits before a stagecoach station in the Wyoming Territory of the late 1860s opens the drama. Another woman, Macon Hill, enters and, seeing Bess, says, "Lord Almighty. . . . You're like me" (5). Macon, who is an outgoing, giving woman, shares her food with the hungry Bess. As they converse, they learn that they have much in common. Both come from a repressive or denigrating background: Bess cannot remember being prepared in school for an independent existence after school and Macon was considered the "runt" in her family of "large-bodied people" (7). The two are attracted to the West's "boundlessness" (5); more striking, they are both mail-order brides.

The conversation establishes the West as a metaphor for opportunities, denied to them in the culture of submissiveness from which they come, for them to develop as women. The time is important. *Abundance* covers twenty-five years, but by beginning the action in the late 1860s, Henley restricts the number of women adventurous enough to pursue the opportunities to two. Hence Macon's surprise at seeing another adventurous soul like herself. The time period also is significant in that women in the late 1860s were generally still dependent on men; they needed the security and protection of marriage in order to proceed in their ventures.

Though the minimal setting and the episodic scenes remove naturalism from the mode of production, the play's conversation and situation retain naturalism's deterministic meaning. Men still perceive women naturalistically, a perception that engenders a different attitude in each woman. Macon is initially the more rebellious in that she will not allow the patriarchal culture to determine her identity or her destiny. As she understands herself, her talent is imagination, her faculty for inventing images, and the images are unrelated to women's repressed or denigrated collective history and her own individual history. Coming to the West, she has severed her connection to the past. "But out here I can be whoever I want. Nobody knows me. I'm gonna make everything up as I go." This "whole new experience" (7) she plans someday to put in the form of a novel. Bess is initially the more docile of the two women. Lacking Macon's self-confidence, she has a more traditional goal. She wants to create a marriage fructified by the love that infuses the stories she has read about "princesses and chimney sweeps and dragon slayers" (7). To her marriage she will bring, in addition to the capacity for love, the talent she possesses: her gift of singing. Her hopes are high because the man who sent her partial fare for her journey westward impresses her in his correspondence with his sensitivity to the expanse of sky and his appreciation of singing.

This kind of marriage, one in which she would be a contributing partner whose talent would creatively shape the marriage, is denied to women in the culture in which they are expected to submit to male authority. It is denied to Bess and Macon on the West's frontier too because the women do not know themselves. Their dreams are fantasies: aspirations separated from a ground in the real world and in themselves. Bess' hope, for instance, is the stuff of storybook romance, not the reality of androcentric marriage. Thus the fantasies are deflated as soon as the men arrive. Jack Flan announces himself as the brother of the man Bess was expecting to marry, who was killed in an accident. Jack will marry her on condition that she stop being a "woman alright" (8) by curbing the tendency to cry. To assure her that he is serious, he knocks her down, and Macon also when she tries to intervene. Promising not to cry, Bess gets up and leaves with him. Macon too leaves with her man, the one-eyed Will Curtis, as the first scene ends.

The remaining scenes of act 1 dramatize the changes in the two women that precede the gap between acts 1 and 2. The change is first noticeable in Macon, for it was she who informed the other woman at the stagecoach station that her coming west signaled her readiness for "some sweeping changes" (6) in her life. She foresees these changes coming through her exploration of the exterior world, whether the exploration is real or invented, and she sees herself equal to the challenge. "I like giving gifts. It's who I am" (15), she says, waving away Bess's promise to repay the coffee and shoes she gives her. She is generous and enthusiastic, but she does not know herself. Not satisfied with her marriage to Will, within six months she proposes to her friend that they press farther into the West, but Bess declines because she is trying to make her marriage to Jack work and because the journey is fraught with danger. Macon therefore does not leave, but by staying she discovers her ability to manage the ranch so that she and Will prosper. She also discovers her sexual attraction to Jack, who makes his desire known to her, though she resists her feelings and his advances.

As act 1 unfolds, Macon discovers what was undeveloped in her when the play opened. She has a practical nature and a sexual nature. Bess came to the West to experience love. Macon, who came for the adventure, tossed off as "hunting down the elephant" (7), accepted Will's proposal only because she had to as a condition of the adventure. Yet she realizes that she is not ready to press on alone. If Bess will not go with her, she will not go, and although she cannot quench her attraction to her friend's husband, she will not surrender to it either. On the evening the two couples celebrate their fourth wedding anniversary, she removes combs from her hair and asks Jack to hold them while she dances. She is alone later when he grabs her, but their "*terrible passion*" (32) for each other notwithstanding, she tells him that she will not betray her friend.

Bess begins to change as she begins to lose faith in that which brought her to the West: her desire to experience love. Her marriage does not work because of Jack's method for dominating women. Denying them a spiritual nature, he reduces them to either kitchen drudges or bedroom playthings. Despite her desire to be a "good wife, patient and submissive" (7), Bess is but an incompetent drudge. "She's good at scrubbing dishes, but all her cakes fall flat as nickels" (26), Jack ridicules her in front of the other couple. No matter how hard she tries, therefore, she cannot please him—so that following the death of their baby, she is ready to press farther into the West, but Macon, who earlier promised to go but who is enjoying entrepreneurship, stalls. While the would-be novelist gains a stronger sense of herself, the would-be wife and mother loses her sense of herself; her husband's aversion and their baby's death, which Jack blames on her, crumble Bess's fragile self-confidence. Yet her readying herself to go farther westward indicates her distancing herself from male authority. She is psychologically readying herself for subjectivity.

On the eve of her disappearance, Bess's self is all but annihilated. As the two couples celebrate their anniversary, Jack and Macon cannot conceal the chemistry between them. Neither can Bess conceal her clumsiness attempting to dance or her incompetence as a cook. And her one talent upon her arrival in the West, singing, has atrophied. She stops when she realizes that she has forgotten the words. "It felt funny opening up my throat to sing," she apologizes. "Like it was somebody else who was singing. Somebody else who wasn't me" (29). Having lost her sense of self, she leaves the cabin to pick flowers. Concerned about her, Macon starts to leave to bring her back, but Will goes instead. Act 1 ends with Will returning with Bess's cape and an

Indian arrow. Apparently the Oglala tribe kidnaps her because, despite search parties, articles in broadsides, and inquiries, her whereabouts are unknown for five years until a Mexican fur trader notifies the Army, which buys her from the chief of the tribe with whom she is living.

Two interpretations of the missing years obtain. The first is the version Bess tells Macon and presumably narrates in a book that she writes. She, however, is the sole source of information about these five years. The letter informing the others of her imminent return merely states that the Mexican trader notified the military, which reclaimed her. Furthermore, since no scenes in the play depict her reading from her book or addressing an audience on the lecture circuit where she is in demand, as the short story writer turned novelist does in Donald Margulies's *Collected Stories*, the play's audience cannot be sure about Bess's book's contents beyond an occasional reference to Indian captivity.

Yet her chin is tattooed, a ceremonial ritual she claims to have undergone to be the chief's bride. For Macon, who remains loyal to her, she returns "from the vale of death. Fresh from pandemonium" (35). To "wean her from her savage ways" (38), her friend has her chained to a stake to prevent her from running away, although Bess does not say where she intends to go. The tribe does not seem to be her destination. She does not pine for her Indian husband. Not only did he sell her to the Army, he sold her "cheap. . . . Cheap" (37). Neither does she exhibit any grief over her separation from the two children she tells Macon she had by the chief. This detail casts doubt on the first version of Bess's years away. It is the second instance in the play of a variation on the rejected or neglected child motif from Henley's plays of the 1980s, a motif that gains in intensity in those plays from Ashbe's being left home alone through Teddy's miscarriage and Sue Jack's confession of negligence. The first instance in *Abundance* is consistent with this progression of intensity: in act 1, Bess teetered on the brink of madness over the death of her child by Jack, dressing her prairie dog in a bonnet and shawl and "rocking it on the porch, talking to it just like it was a somebody" (17), as Will described her derangement. Yet the second instance is not consistent. That she suffers no sense of loss of her Indian children—she never again even mentions them to any of the other characters—suggests that they do not exist. If they do, her sojourn in savagery not only dissolved her civilized precepts, it obliterated her maternal instinct.

A second detail also casts doubt on this first version. In the story she relates, a chief selected her to be his bride, she bore him two children, and in one of her few references to the contents of the book she wrote, her singing transformed the savages into "charmed wolves" (42). The fulfillment of a desire thwarted with Jack suggests a conscious construction, a fabrication, on her part. The gift her husband rejected was one the Oglalas accepted. Her singing enthralled them.

The second version requires two paragraphs of introduction. Returned to civilization, Bess is unresponsive until Jack and Will leave the cabin, at which time she speaks to Macon, shares a laugh with her, and tells her about her marriage to the Indian chief and the two children she had with him. Jack returns and with Will not present and his wife of no consequence, he grabs Macon, who resists. She sends him out of the cabin and apologizes to her friend for his behavior by explaining that she will not allow him to approach her that way again—he did only because they thought she was dead. In other words, they became intimate after her disappearance.

Bess, however, disagrees. She reminds Macon that on the night the two couples celebrated their fourth wedding anniversary, her friend removed the combs from her hair before dancing but asked Jack, not her own husband, to hold them for her. As Bess interpreted the interaction, Macon was proposing intimacy while she and Jack were living with Macon and Will following the destruction of their cabin. And that was the night she was apparently kidnapped, though in the penultimate scene of act 1, which takes place early in the day of the anniversary, Henley foreshadows her leaving. Arguing for that night, Bess entreats Macon: "Please, I can't stay here no longer. . . . We got t' go now. You promised. You swore." But Macon is equally insistent: "Stop pushing at me. I got things here" (25).

Following the reminder of that night, Bess stops speaking and attempts to run away, forcing Macon to have her chained, until a Professor Elmore Crome arrives. He has read about her ordeal in a broadside and would like to write a book with her; he argues that people would buy such a book to learn about "Indian ways . . . their lives . . . their treachery." To everyone's surprise she speaks. She can write such a book "about treachery" (41). The implication, of course, is that she is responding to the treachery of her husband and friend, against whom she retaliates. Now that she is a celebrity, she reverses her relationships with them. She reduces Jack to a kept man, although he does not object to being a lackey, since he does not have to get a job and he is taken care of. She denies financial help to Macon and Will, whose fortunes have so suffered a reversal that the bank is repossessing their property, and she taunts Macon about not writing the narrative that she has written: a book with sales that make it a "phenomenon" (44).

The second version actualizes the West as a metaphor, the westward journey as an archetypal journey. Henley situates the drama in a place not yet charted, so to speak, because Wyoming in the late 1860s had just been made a territory but had not yet been granted statehood—in act 1, reference is made to new land opened up for homesteaders—and at a time when traveling would have been perilous for unescorted women. The farther a woman travels into this West the more her opportunities for self-discovery increase—but so do the risks, because she may discover something about herself that conflicts with her self-image. Macon, who journeys as far as the frontier, gains practical managerial skills and knowledge of her sexual nature while losing her interest in writing a novel. Bess, who penetrates the interior, gains a self while losing her loving nature, and the self she gains is the one Macon lost.

The most fruitful approach to the second version explaining Bess's disappearance is through the playwright's technique of repeating, with variations, images from earlier plays. For example, Bess's feeling "so empty" in act 1 that she "eat[s] warm mud, trying to fill up the craving," (22) recalls Bliss's figurative "hole," in *The Debutante Ball,* for her "desperate longing to love and be loved" (306). Sue Jack and Carnelle, however, are the two characters in Henley's naturalistic plays whose experiences Bess's own experience develops. Trying to get Hooker to understand that she changed during her time in prison, Sue Jack relates how she would stare at a photo of herself that she could not recognize because the "girl in the picture" had departed "so unknowingly, so unexpectedly" (231). In the final scene, she tells him that she was "out walking. And thinking" (261) about him, and that admission is followed by her recognition that although she does not yet know how to be, she knows she can be a new self. But this new self is in the future; in the present she reunites with her husband in a loving relationship. Similarly, in an attempt to win Bess's trust, the professor brings her a gift, a mirror in which she sees herself presumably for the first time since her disappearance because she "*touches the tattoos on her chin*" as she looks. She also presumably thinks about his appeal to her to write her story, in addition to five years of thinking about her relationship with her husband, because she does not respond until Jack orders him to leave, and then to everyone's surprise she agrees to "write book" (41). In the mirror image, she recognizes a new self she can be in the present.

Bess's self-discovery recalls as well Carnelle's in a scene from *The Miss Firecracker Contest* not yet discussed. That play opens on Carnelle looking into a mirror before turning to the audience to practice her routine for the contest's talent segment: a combination of dancing, marching, and baton twirling performed to "The Star Spangled Banner." She stops periodically to record her "*ideas in her notebook*" (147). Ostensibly trying to integrate the various components of the routine, such as when to ignite the roman candle, she is actually trying to impose her image of her new self onto reality: her reality as Carnelle Scott and the contest's reality. "I think that'll work" (147), she muses, and she spends much of the play trying to make her idea—her image—work. "That's what I wanted, crimson red" (154), she answers Elain's surprise at seeing the dyed hair. She needs her cousin's red dress because she has made "crimson red" her "thematic color" (157) for the contest. If she wins, she tells Delmount, she can leave Brookhaven "in a crimson blaze of glory!" (163). "I love the color red. I love how it blazes!" (187) she defends her choice of image to Elain. Yet she not only loses, she places fifth in a field of five, so she has to accept the fact that the image does not work, which she does in her final scene, which begins with her telling Mac Sam that following the parade she was "out walking by the railroad tracks" by herself and "thinking" (201).

Disappointed by the contest's outcome, she asks him what one can reasonably hope for in life, to which he replies, "There's always eternal grace" (202). The reply does not inspire her because it is so far removed from her everyday existence. Declining the invitation of Popcyc and Delmount to watch the fireworks with them on the roof of the tent, she looks into the mirror and sees her hair as brown; she sees herself as she was before she tried to impose her false image on reality. This scene is not a gap in the action, but it is different from self-discovery scenes in Henley's other naturalistic plays. In these, the heroine withdraws, by putting her head in an oven or going off to walk by herself, and returns to talk with someone close to her. Carnelle's looking at herself in the mirror after walking and talking is an inchoate attempt at depicting the interior journey. While she is in this reflective state, above her Popeye, relating her experience at the observatory, repeats the attendant's remark about the mind's ability to actualize that which it can imagine. The remark impinges on her consciousness, and she makes the connection with Mac Sam's remark: "Grace. Eternal grace. Grace." Joining the two on the roof, she is "*ablaze with excitement*" as the imagery reverses the pattern in the preceding scenes.

Neither the color of her hair nor that of her dress can create the crimson blaze of glory in which Carnelle wanted to leave Brookhaven. She makes no attempt to record her ideas in her notebook because she is not receiving ideas; she is receiving a surge of power. The fire that transforms, the current that creates, is within her. Admitting that she does not have the "vaguest idea" of the "main thing" is her epiphany that she cannot force a new self into existence, but that instead it issues from the interaction of imagination with the self that is and the world that is. Imagination can change her life, for the explosion of colors in the sky is a stage image of the exploding imagination as the light from the fireworks, bursting from gold to red to "crimson red," floods their faces. Esemplastic imagination integrates the self and the world, creating a new self. "Gosh, it's a nice night" (203–4), the heroine enjoys a magical moment with her cousin and her friend.[2]

Carnelle is the only major character in the plays of the 1980s to discover the imagination rather than love as the source of identity. But she does not act on the discovery; the audience does not see her using her awakened imagination. The audience sees and hears Bess using hers, however. During the years she was missing, she turned inward to discover a voice with which to tell her story, needing only the stimulus of the professor to tell it. In telling her story, however fragmented, she brings her process of self-discovery into the view of the audience. Thus does this action overcome Jonnie Guerra's criticism of Henley's theater, an excerpt of which is quoted in chapter 2. Writing in the 1980s, Guerra found a "weakness in Henley's portrayal of female quest" in the offstage withdrawal into the self for the discovery that the heroine announces upon her return. Because "telling does not substitute for showing," this weakness ostensibly results from the playwright's reliance upon traditional, nonfeminist dramaturgy. Another weakness, "perhaps the most damning criticism of Henley's treatment of the quest," is that "she never completes the 're-visioning' of her women characters' lives." The heroines arrive at the threshold of transformation but do not cross it into restructured lives.[3]

Abundance does not have a stage image representing the heroine's interior self, her inner life, and Henley's theater does not offer any such image until *Control Freaks*, but it does have images that issue from Bess's self-discovery. By not dramatizing the missing five years, which would follow traditional dramaturgy, Henley takes an innovative, experimental approach not seen in *The Miss Firecracker Contest* and has Bess empower herself by telling her story of those years. Her telling proves she discovered herself, for her story is her imagination in action: the images that actualize her experience. The strategy works. She crosses the threshold, as Carnelle does not, to live a new life. That Bess creates a new self with her awakened imagination attests to Henley's development as an artist, and that Bess creates a nontraditional narrative with her awakened imagination attests to Henley's growth beyond the naturalistic plays.

In their studies of avant-garde, alternative, and postmodern theater and fiction, Arnold Aronson, Theodore Shank, and Elizabeth Deeds Ermarth isolate three characteristics that the critic can find in *Abundance*, the first play in a decade of Henley's plays that this study prefers to call experimental. These three eliminate or subvert traditional linear narrative, eliminate an unambiguous frame of reference within a work to guide the spectator or reader, and engage the spectator or reader in a creative process that accommodates multilevel thinking and parallel possibilities.[4]

For the critic who wants an unambiguous interpretation of Bess's disappearance, the two versions can be reconciled in that the second version explains how Bess gained the self that enables her to tell the first. Any contradiction would be resolved—that is, were it not for the Henleyan technique of repeating images, which this study has examined from play to play. *The Miss*

Firecracker Contest also prepares for *Abundance* by repeating within the play a color image, from the red hair to the crimson red in the pyrotechnical display: varying repetitions that alter the heroine's perception. *Abundance,* too, repeats images within the play—but in a pattern that disturbs the spectator's perception.

Bess discovers a voice in captivity, but it is Macon's voice; in retaliation for Macon's appropriating her role with Jack, she appropriates her friend's voice. The first occurrence comes in act 2, in a scene in which she reveals the existence of two children. To Macon's comment about her ability to survive, she says that she was able to by picturing her, Macon. Clarifying, she adds, "Hunt the elephant. . . . Bang, bang, bang" (36). The words are immediately recognizable by the audience as repeating those Macon spoke at the stagecoach station when she declared her aspiration to be a novelist, but it took the publication of the text of *Abundance* to document the frequency with which Henley repeats images or phrases. It pervades Bess's references to the missing five years. She is downright vindictive in some passages, such as the following. In front of Macon and Jack, she tells the professor that she survived by hunting "for wild fruits that grow all in abundance" (42) on the terrain. The words repeat those Macon spoke (15) in act 1 to Bess's question about their ability to survive should they leave their husbands to press farther west. Then to add insult to injury, Bess whistles. It was Macon who taught her to whistle and who whistled at the mute, tattooed woman in the hope of establishing communication with her after her return. Bess is transformed. The woman who could do nothing right in act 1 has a voice—"Like an angel!" (42) exclaims the professor—to write a book and travel about the country on a lecture tour. Yet when she speaks about herself and her Oglala experience, the images are Macon's originally spoken more than nine years earlier.

The critic who wants an unambiguous interpretation can neutralize the apparent contradiction in Bess's discovery by seeing her as unsure of herself in actualizing the imagination. Not having had a desire to write a novel, she does not know how to use her discovery. Hence when she discovers her imagination, the images do not flow; they trickle. And since she believes Macon betrayed her, she retaliates by taking Macon's images. Not only do they sound more authentic than her own, they satisfy her desire for revenge.

Yet if this explanation is at first satisfying, the critic then encounters another turn that renders linear action recursive, another ambiguity that envelopes the missing five years, another detail that casts doubt on the second version as the details of Bess's two Indian children and her singing in captivity cast doubt on the first version. Bess taunts the woman who always thought they were friends by repeating the latter's images and expressions until Macon explodes: "You pictured me. You stole from me. You stole me" (47). In a vicious exchange, Bess turns on her former friend and, extending a knife, offers her some advice: "Well, maybe it ain't too late. Maybe you've got one more chance. Here, take this knife. Take this ink. Go ahead. Cut open your face. Pour in the ink. Go be me, if you think you can. If you think you're so brave. I'll let you be me. You can do my tour. People will rise to their feet and clamor for you" (47).

It is difficult to hear this speech in the theater and not consider the possibility that Bess is revealing what she did following her interpretation of Macon's betrayal at the wedding anniversary. The possibility exists that she vanished that night into her heart of darkness, in her rage wandering and wounding herself until she eventually became a member of an Indian tribe, there to remain until the cavalry reclaimed her and while there, her rage having consumed itself, to explore the hole, the emptiness, within herself. The notion of self-disfigurement receives support from a piece of dialogue in the closing scene, which reunites the two women in St. Louis after an interim of fifteen years. Bess, who earlier that day learned of her Indian husband's death, remarks that she regrets not being able to see him again. Macon agrees that life is not ideal as they expected it to be when they first met but that at least she, Bess, "saw the elephant." How Bess delivers her speech in response to the expression signifying the activation of the imagination is critical. If she pauses before repeating, "Yeah," she turns into herself to see the rivers in the colors of her imagination: "Yeah. Yeah, the Oglalas knew such beautiful places. I saw rivers that were so clear you could see every pebble and fish. And the water was any color you could dream: pink and turquoise, gold and white, lime green." Macon's response implies a recognition that the description combines fiction with fact, that some part of the Oglala story is a fabrication: "Hell of a time you had with the Oglalas." Bess then closes the evocation of that period in her life: "Beautiful time I had" (52).

It is not possible to determine exactly what happened during the missing five years. Moreover, a determination is not important. What happened during those years is not important; what Bess makes of what happened is.

The play's opening scene, with Macon coming upon Bess at the stagecoach station and declaring, "Lord Almighty. . . . You're like me" (5), sets the stage for a drama in which the two women are doubles. Each one is capable of the other one's experience. Macon, for example, could have been a writer because the images Bess summons for her book are Macon's. Yet the women do not develop their potentials together. They are closest in sharing their aspirations and reflecting on their lives in the opening and closing scenes, which function as a framework for the drama, and furthest apart in the two missing time periods, the first of five years and the second of fifteen, before the two women reunite in St. Louis. On one level, *Abundance* dramatizes their separation and reconciliation.

When the women arrive in the West, Macon thinks that she has severed her connection to the past, but she is unprepared for Jack's sexual overture and the extent to which her sexual nature will drive her. She resents his changing her name to May Ann, but the maneuver is a familiar one because naming is a male strategy in the culture of submissiveness for asserting dominance over the female. In *The Wake of Jamey Foster,* Wayne prefers to call the widow's sister Charlotte. "I like it better than Collard" (124), he tells her. Unlike Collard, Macon eventually yields.

Twenty-five years after arriving at the frontier, Macon still does not understand. "It's a shame how things turn out," she reflects in the closing scene. "I swear to God, I wish I knew how it could be different." When Bess agrees with her, Macon points out that at least she "saw the elephant" (52), prompting Bess to evoke for a final time the Oglala period of her life. But since Macon does not mention the Oglalas, it is Bess who equates the expression signifying the activation of the imagination with her Indian captivity. To transform her experience, she had to discover herself, and the source of identity, of subjectivity, in this play is the imagination. *Abundance* dramatizes this development for Bess but not for Macon.

Alan Clarke Shepard studies how women in Henley's plays beginning with *Crimes of the Heart* and ending with *The Wake of Jamey Foster* deal with the rage they feel for being abused, betrayed, or abandoned. He traces an arc that begins with their rebellion but that ultimately ends with their aborting their rage and repudiating their rebellion to repatriate themselves into the southern culture in which women are expected to be submissive to male authority. But he also sees them groping "toward liberty" because he perceives the arc in *Crimes of the Heart* to be longer and wider than that in Henley's first play to be staged, *Am I Blue.*[5]

In *Abundance,* though, Bess does not grope; she acts decisively in a key scene in act 2. According to the stage directions for scene 4, a restrained Bess "*jerks violently at her chain. She struggles with fierce rage pounding the chain. She moans with unbearable despair and finally sinks to the ground exhausted*" (40). Were the play to end at this point, she would have traversed the arc that Shepard describes. But the play does not end. Bess is visited by the professor, who gives her a mirror in which she examines her transformed face, touching her skin where it corresponds to the reflection until she recognizes that she can write a book about treachery. The fame that follows the book's publication not only liberates her from male authority but enables her to reduce chauvinist Jack to submission and to direct her rage against Macon. Although in the second instance her retaliation is severe because the latter was her friend, and a generous one, Bess controls her emotions. Macon, in contrast, is controlled by hers as evidenced by her ongoing affair with Jack, who ditches her after he settles into his role as Bess's kept man, for she was never more than a bedroom plaything to him.

All of this unfolds in a play in which the doubling, established in the stagecoach station, is a structural principle. When Bess extends the knife to Macon and challenges her to cut her face, the drama repeats that of the closing scene of act 1, with the situation reversed. Macon feels betrayed. Jack has ended their relationship to stay with his wife; Will is leaving for deeper penetration into the West but does not want her to accompany him because she never loved him; and Bess is taking her images to tell her account of her years in captivity. Yet she does nothing about the situation. The scene ends with her repeating, "Nothing. . . . Nothing" (49). It is followed by a fifteen-year gap before the reconciliation.

In the closing scene, Macon sits alone playing solitaire in a carnival tent—an image that suggests a parallel to at least some portion of Bess's life during the missing years before her return. The parallels continue after Bess joins her. She has a connection with Indians in that she had been selling an "Indian Remedy" (52) for substance abuse. She also has a facial disfigurement caused, according to Jack, who saw her earlier in the day, by a "syphilitic disease" (51). But she has no remedy for her situation because she lacks Bess' subjective self-understanding. As she says to her visitor, "You know, when I was younger, I never knew who I was, what I wanted, where I was going or how to get there. Now that I'm older, I don't know none of that either" (52–53). Macon has not looked at herself in the mirror as her visitor did to recognize that she could transform her experience. Although she had fifteen years in which to journey inward as compared to Bess' five years, she has not developed her imagination or discovered any potential in herself beyond an ability to manage a home and conduct an extramarital affair, two ventures that ultimately fail.

Bess, on the other hand, gains an identity because she explores the unknown in herself. Whether the tale she tells of her five-year experience is real or invented, she transforms it in the exterior world into the identity of "Mrs. Bess Johnson" (49): a married woman who uses her maiden name, Johnson, and not her husband's name, Flan. In a patriarchal culture that expects women to be submissive objects, she plumbs the depth of her being to discover herself as a subject, channeling her rage not against the Oglalas, who allegedly kidnapped her, but against her husband and friend, who betrayed her. The channeled rage invests her with a self and an imagination that in the closing scene releases her own images for the landscape of the interior journey in a passage, already quoted, that begins, "I saw rivers that were so clear," and that contains the colors of a dreamscape. The colors do not explode as they do in the fireworks display that closes *The Miss Firecracker Contest,* but what they lack in pyrotechnical brilliance they make up for in generative power. Carnelle basks in the imagination's power as the colors flood her face. Bess actualizes the power by delivering the colors, and though they do not flood, they have increased in intensity from the trickle at the opening of act 2. The passage also shows that she has purged herself of any lingering rancorous feelings. Without this passage, her development apes that of an egomaniacal male such as Jack and aggrandizes her self through the appropriation of the contents, such as images, of other selves. But with the Oglala story losing its drawing power on the lecture circuit so that she no longer needs the professor's services as secretary-manager, she hears of her Indian husband's death and Macon's affliction and is able to think of someone other than herself. Liberated to release the images that express her deepest self, she can be friends with the woman who was her companion on the frontier of the women's movement.

Returning to the past before their separation, the two women share a magical moment as they "*laugh from deep in the bottom of their hearts*" (53), but they do so on the day that Bess surrenders her claim to the story that separated them. When earlier that day her manager reads from a newspaper review that her latest talk seemed "outdated" (50), Bess is relieved not to have to go on telling the same story over and over. Despite her having achieved a national reputation with the story, they decide to disband their union because it is time for a change. Only when she surrenders that claim, that engagement, can she reclaim love, the engagement in a relationship with her companion on the interior, westward journey she has been rejecting in act 2. Thus the closing scene foreshadows the major conflict that marks Henley's plays of the new decade.

With its discovery of the imagination as a source of identity and its experimentation with nontraditional dramaturgy, *Abundance* is the bellwether play of the 1990s as *Crimes of the Heart* is the bellwether play of the 1980s. At the end of her first decade of writing, Henley felt the need for a change. Introducing the second volume of the collected edition, she explains that *The Lucky Spot* and *Abundance* "are plays written about parts of my life that occurred after leaving Mississippi" but that her next play, *Signature,* is different: "After completing two plays that had required a lot of research, I was anxious to write something completely from my imagination with no concern for history or fact."[6]

The time of *Signature* is the future: 2052. The place is Los Angeles "in some form of Hollywood." The prepositional phrases make the setting more image than substance; light and sound rather than furniture, for example, set a scene. The description is that of clashing opposites, for the effect is a "strange, chaotically horrifying, deathly beautiful, sadly silly world."[7] In separate studies, Janet V. Haedicke compares *Crimes of the Heart* with Sam Shepard's *A Lie of the Mind* and Karen L. Laughlin compares *Abundance* with his *True West.*[8] *Signature* might be compared with Shepard's *Angel City,* for both take place in a futuristic Hollywood beset by smog and other environmental disorders in which characters suffer body sores.

The opening scene of Henley's play introduces four of the play's five adult characters. Boswell T-Thorp is a conceptual artist, an inventor of the Box Theory that enjoyed a vogue some years earlier. As he explains to his brother Maxwell, he is practicing meeting other guests at the party to which he is going that evening, the Celebrity Chase, because even though he "suffer[s] around the social scene" (59), both know that to be successful in Hollywood, one must be seen at celebrity events. The play calls for a rectangle or square that could be used the same way as is the rectangle in *Angel City.* In the Shepard play, when the actors appear behind the rectangle and are framed by it, it becomes a screen and they become images in a movie that the other actors watch. While the brothers are talking in Henley's play, the television phone in Boswell's apartment bleeps and a woman's image appears on the rectangle, which becomes a screen as they telecommunicate. If the segment is not videotaped, the performer could appear behind the rectangle and be framed by it, as interns did when the play had its first workshop production.[9] The woman whose image appears is L-Tip, Boswell's manager and Max's wife, who is divorcing him. Not only is she too going to the party, she secured passes for the main floor.

Identifying himself as an inventor and an "art philosopher" (63), Boswell sees himself creating images with which to conceptualize abstractions such as the Box Theory, the poster for which won him the Grand Poster Prize. He dresses to reflect that past glory. As the play opens, he "*puts on a square shirt, a square tie, square shoes, a square wig, a square belt, and so forth*" (59). As L-Tip sees herself, she creates images with her clients and her person. For the party she impersonates Pansy Martin, a popular fantasy puppet on television. "*She is dressed in an array of ghastly colored flowers. Strange antennas poke out of her head-dress*" (60–61). Both speak a language unique to this brave new world. "Tab some ear fuel and dust" (59), Boswell tells Max to leave the apartment. "God, you are so brill" (62), thrills L-Tip to her client's achievement with his Box Theory.

The fourth character enters the apartment during the scene. A woman named William, she is Boswell's tenant. A hanger-on in the celebrity culture, he is forced to take in a tenant to pay his bills, and she is forced to be a tenant because she is a government employee who cannot afford her own place. Her job description is removing splatter from animals caught in the recurring environmental convulsions. In a subsequent scene, the audience learns that the convulsions are so recurring and so destructive that the government has divided the work force into four crews to attend to the four major types of environmental disaster: quake, spill, burn, and splatter. The convulsions take their toll on the ecology. When Boswell returns from the party, William asks him what food was served, the implication being that workers cannot expect much variety in their meals. A sausage on Sunday, for example, is a treat that William enjoys. The convulsions also affect people. Boswell is dying from an unnamed illness; by act 1, scene 5, the "*smog is thick and green and brown*" (73), and by the sixth scene, "*grey sores are visible on his chest*" (74).

The four characters are paired in a fashion similar to how Bliss and Frances and Jen and Teddy in *The Debutante Ball* are paired. Max and William could be characters in the naturalistic plays in that their need to love and be loved gives them their identity. L-Tip's appointment with Video Divorce so devastates

Max that he implores his brother to explain what happened to their marriage. "Because, you see, I love her so much. Oh, why can't she love me?! What made her stop loving me?!" (59). In a later scene, she gives him a reason, but it does not satisfy him. Nothing but reconciliation can satisfy him, and to that end he grovels before her, verbally abuses her, writes poetry for her—to no avail. When she finally gets him to understand that their marriage is over, he voluntarily submits himself to the state's euthanasia program. Even though his poetry confers recognition, which he enjoys in the celebrity culture, he cannot live without love. Neither will he seek another partner, for he does not subscribe to the notion that his "profound love" can be "replaced, or forgotten, or lived without" (95). His ex-wife calls him immature and a charlatan posing as a lovesick poet to increase sales of his poetry, but he does not withdraw from the program. Having discovered that his interiority can be filled by nothing but love, its rejection nullifies the adulation art gives him. His self-images throughout the play are those of isolation and diminution. He would rather be dead than "alone on the parched, dry shore," and without L-Tip's love, he cannot go back to her "always hoping for its return like sawed off legs that will never grow back" (95–96). The reason he gives for the "euth request" is a "broken heart" (80).

William is the character with whom Max is paired. In body language and direct statement, she lets Boswell know her feelings. When he returns from the Celebrity Chase, she gets out of bed, prepares his medicine, and sits on her mat "*hugging herself with both arms.*" Granted permission to move closer to him, on his mat with folded arms, she "*slowly leans over and sets her head on his shoulder*" as he itemizes the food served at the party (66). "I don't want you to die" (72), she tries to comfort him when tests confirm the seriousness of his illness. Yet when he terminates their relationship, temporarily dashing her hope for a home to which she can bring her two children, frozen in suspension until she can meet the conditions for defrosting them, she does not volunteer for the euthanasia program. Her self-discovery is imaged visually. Unable to persuade Max not to volunteer, she continues removing splatter in the space she rents in Boswell's apartment. She brings work home with her to enhance her performance and thereby qualify for greater worker benefits such as more living space. As telecommunicating Max supplies the information for his euth request, she lifts from her workstation and rocks a creature on which she labored; it is "*clean and pink and glowing*" (80). She discovers that her interiority is filled with love whether or not it is reciprocated.

L-Tip and Boswell develop from characterizations in *Abundance*. Minus the generosity, L-Tip is a contemporary Macon, the woman who, despite her motivation for taking a journey, settles instead into entrepreneurship and who, despite her avowal that she will tolerate a man only so long as she needs him, settles into an illicit relationship with Bess's husband. L-Tip experienced a self-discovery prior to the opening scene, and what she discovered was that having a career in the celebrity culture would be more fulfilling than vicariously living the glamour and excitement by having fantasy products. "I'm a professional woman," she identifies herself to William. "All my dreams are coming true" (77). A former housewife and clerk at a noodle stand, she filed for divorce and became a manager of celebrities. To get started, she took on Boswell as her first client because as the inventor of the Box Theory, he once was a celebrity. Their professional relationship is short-lived, despite her proposal of a sexual relationship, an offer he declines because he is under surveillance. He wants her to organize a memorial in his honor, an impossible task, she argues, for someone who is not marketable. With five new clients, she quickly recovers from his firing her.

L-Tip cannot understand Max's decision to have himself euthanized, especially since he has become a celebrity. "Why, you could find a new love tomorrow. Or perhaps even tonight" (95), she tells him. She herself finds a new partner. She marries her leading client, not for love but as a "career move," and she does not expect the marriage to "work out" (78), a prophecy that comes true. "Trend is life" (77) is her motto; doing "anything to get out ahead" (78) is her modus operandi.

Similarly, Boswell is a contemporary Bess, for whom imagination confers identity—but whose identity is mired in the art created in the past and who clings to her one story long after there is an audience for it. William, some twenty years his junior, admits to L-Tip that she "never even heard of Boxdom" (77) before moving into his apartment. Yet that is the way he wants to be known. "I'm Boswell L-Thorp," he rehearses for the Celebrity Chase. "The Box Theory? Yes, that was mine. I invented it. It came from me" (59). His mindset puts him in conflict with L-Tip, the representative of a culture that idolizes current celebrities, who are the trendsetters. For her, he is a has-been, and because he has "been out of orbit for a very long time," the best that she can get for him is an alternate slot, in case a scheduled guest cancels, on "The Whatever Happened To Show." And though he protests that his integrity, his refusal to be a "grinning, glad-handing salt lick for the press," kept him out of orbit (63–64), he succumbed to another temptation. Disputing L-Tip's criticism in a later scene that he stopped creating after the Boxdom success, he counters, "I made replica posters, sold souvenir boxes" (77), his choice of words ironically substantiating her charge.

Were his living in the past his sole characteristic, Boswell could be a stock character in comedy or an object of pity. Yet he is neither funny nor sympathetic because he is mean-spirited with Max, as Bess is with Macon, and obnoxious. In his division of labor, he is the creative artist and his brother is the worker who supports both of them, an arrangement that the latter accepts. When Max is fired, however, he turns to Boswell, begging for help: "I'm homeless. I could use anything. A tin cup. A cardboard box." But the inventor of the Box Theory denies him the needed help: "I don't want to. I don't have any time. You have to go" (70). As for his obnoxiousness, he is condescending with William: "You with your non-skilled job. . . . A mindless job, unglamorous, unrewarding, unbearably dull and useless" (71).

How Henley writes the four characters to relate to her obsessive images and motifs completes her picture of them. Irritated by Max imploring him to explain L-Tip's divorce action since he still loves her, Boswell mocks his brother's anguish, denigrating love to a "tawdry reflection of all the holes in your own shredded soul" (60). Although Max does not use the metaphor, he would agree with Marshael in *The Wake of Jamey Foster* that her spouse abandoning her left a hole in her being. Boswell combines the metaphor with the image of the mirror. Love does not fill the hole, as it does for characters in the naturalistic plays, giving them a sense of self-worth and connecting them with other characters. Love is a mirror in which one sees the holes in oneself; love renders one vulnerable by making one aware of needs, fears, whatever the holes are meant to suggest. For Boswell, imagination fills the hole or holes, conferring self-worth;

expressed as art, imagination connects the creator with an appreciative audience such as the audience he had for Boxdom.

The motif of the neglected or rejected child appears throughout the play as well. In the closing scene, L-Tip tells William that she has a daughter, but since she is competing in a world "completely consumed with constructing careers," she does not "have time for a full-term child." She has a Toss 'Em Toddler, bred for careerists, whose life span does not exceed three years. Since this breed is "tossed naturally after three years, the mother does not have to endure the child's testing her independence, her "awkward years," or the "high cost" of her "education" (106). L-Tip is presented here and elsewhere in strokes so broad that the treatment is farcical. In an earlier scene, she arrives at Boswell's apartment "*looking more trendy and today than ever*" (76). Wearing a dress decorated with food, designed for careerists too busy to take time out from tight schedules who must eat on the go, she eats grapes from it while balking at Boswell's proposal for a retrospective and after he leaves shares a meal from it with William.

No matter what outfit William wears, and in most of the scenes she is dressed in a splatterer uniform, she is not treated with such excess. Time permitting, she clicks in on her two children frozen in suspension, reading to them to maintain a subliminal connection until the family can be reunited. She has a purpose in life, she tells Max when he volunteers for the euthanasia program: "I want a home to live in and I want my kids out of F.D. Then I want us all to learn to read and write and clap to music" (80). By play's end she is beginning to achieve her purpose. Elected Worker of the Year, she has secured her own place to live, has her children with her and undergoing defrosting, and has rescued a boy turned loose on the streets by Boswell whom she has declared her ward.

Not confined to the women characters, the neglected child motif appears in two scenes involving Boswell. In the first, he is sorting through memorabilia and talking to himself about how L-Tip can use the materials to promote him when the television phone rings. Expecting L-Tip, he does not recognize the caller, who has to identify herself as "Jennifer T-Thorp. One of your daughters. The middle one," an identification at which he mutters, "Shit. One of my swarmy brats" (75). The girl wants to visit with a present she has for him, but he tells her to laser it to him because he is too busy to see her. Annoyed by the interruption, he is also annoyed by William's presence cleaning splatter from a creature. When she defends working in the space she rents so that she can be reunited with her children, he advises her to "forget about those kids." She is "lucky" not to have to put up with them (76). In the second scene, he defends returning his ward to the government over William's objection that the boy will be remanded to the streets. "He'll be no worse off than he was before" (101) is the art philosopher's dismissal of the issue. Reduced to alternate status on a nostalgia show because instead of developing as an artist he replicated his early success, he withdraws into his past accomplishment and thereby compounds his predicament because trying to relive that accomplishment further isolates him.

Distraught by his reduction to insignificance—by the exterior world not acknowledging his identity—and dying, Boswell lets a graphologist talk him into having his handwriting read, an analysis that chills rather than comforts. "Shallow, self-absorbed, antisocial, conceited, cruel, and cowardly" (82) is the analysis of his writing in the scene that closes act 1. How can I be significant? he asks. Change your handwriting to reflect the new you, she answers. He tries because he wants to "leave" his "signature" as a testimony to his life, and when she approves the change, he writes, "Here lies one whose name was drilled in granite" (83). The critic does not have to speculate about seeing an autobiographical dimension in this scene, for Henley supplies it. In the introduction to *Signature,* she relates how her encounter with a graphologist provided the inspiration for the play. Grief-stricken by the analysis of her writing as talentless and then angry with herself for letting a stranger interpret her "signature . . . essence . . . mark on the world," she rebutted the reading with the epitaph by which she wants to be remembered: "Here lies one whose name was drilled in granite." Jolted from the quietude of not having "written for some time," she "started the play" (viii). Changing her style of writing, she changes the content of the drama's self-discovery to reflect her change in style, thereby continuing the theme and the conflict introduced in *Abundance.* The theme is that art, like love, renders life significant; the conflict pits art against love.

Theme and conflict unfold in a universe increasingly absurd in Henley's experimental plays. Boswell's cynical response to William's justification for her job, that she saves some creatures, is "Saved for what? A miserable life in a filth-filled world. One percent of one splatter is cleaned up before there is a whole new splat out" (71). And even if some are saved, every living thing's ultimate splat out is death. "Oblivion" (72) is his encroaching future, for his medical report gives him less than a year of life. Since he thinks of himself as an artist, he perceives an extra burden "of a mind, an imagination, and a trembling heart" (72); as he lies awake at night, he can picture the void awaiting him. Since he is an art philosopher who invents images that conceptualize abstractions, he compounds the absurdity by conceiving of Boxdom as putting a "box around anything: a circle, a rectangle, a triangle, a moving spill!" (62). He would nullify death by boxing it in.

Critic Miriam M. Chirico is right that Boswell trusts the graphologist who reads his handwriting "because she taps into his greatest fear: his transience."[10] His sores are not symbolic of repressed secrets, as they are with Jen in *The Debutante Ball.* He is a dying man who knows he is dying and is forthright, though unpleasantly, even despicably, so, with his brother, manager, and tenant. His relationship with William plots the conflict. In the first of their three scenes together in act 1, he allows her to prepare his medicine, sit next to him, and set her head on his shoulder as he itemizes the food served at the Celebrity Chase. Alternately domineering and condescending in their second scene, he rejects her attempt to move closer to him. In their third scene, he tells her he is sick of her bringing work home with her. The arrival of L-Tip, whom he addresses as "Darling" (76) before firing her for balking at his proposal of a retrospective, clarifies his increasing annoyance with William. Her solicitous concern for his welfare only exacerbates his condition by focusing attention on his deteriorating health, and her presence distracts him from his mission, ensuring the honoring of the legacy by which he wants to be remembered: Boxdom.

Thus act 1 puts in place the opposing forces in the conflict. Boswell knows he is dying, but death is not what he fears. His fear is that he will die before he can complete his mission. A variation on the naturalistic perception prevalent in Henley's plays of the 1980s, his fear is that he will die without having changed the perception of him as a has-been. His energy in act 1 is directed toward ensuring the Boxdom legacy, but by the end of the act, he has to accept the dearth of interest in his former renown. Hence his meeting with the graphologist excites him because she offers the hope of change. "Then it's not too late?" (83), he asks. The play's ultimate opposition is not art versus encroaching death. Love is art's opposing force because in the dwindling time left to Boswell, it competes with art for his redirected energy.

Although imagination is a "burden" (72) for the stricken man in that he can picture the void awaiting him, it is valuable because it supplies him with images with which to create art. Love is also a burden in that it heightens his awareness of the void and it distracts. It is of no value, however, because it does not supply him with anything he needs. The graphologist, known as Reader, tells him otherwise. Fighting a losing battle with his health and his mission, Boswell lets Reader evaluate his signature in the double sense of calligraphic merit and legacy, both of which she finds lacking. Yet he should not despair. Changing his signature, he can change his life; he can create a new legacy that people will honor. Boswell plunges into the revised mission, trying to pack his head with information about the universe and, in his effort "to reach out to the human species" (85), taking in a ward. When Reader rejects the new handwriting as "swill" (86), she assigns him a program of studying pickles, which he does with enthusiasm but without her praise, for his inadequate writing reflects his continuingly inadequate self. "You're not whole," she tells him. "You're incomplete." The "something" that is missing is a "beloved" (90–91). This incompleteness is a variation on the hole metaphor. He does not feel the incompleteness as Bliss and Frances do in *The Debutante Ball,* but since he trusts Reader's judgment and wants to create a poster comparable to the one that brought him his former renown and therefore ensure his legacy, he designates William his beloved.

Henley's dramaturgical sense does not desert her whether she is creating naturalistic dramas or experimental ones. What happens between two images or scenes is crucial in understanding the change that occurs subsequently in the repeated image or scene. What happens in scene 8 of *Signature,* in which Boswell brings Reader up to date on his situation, is crucial in understanding the conflict in Henley's plays of the 1990s generally as well as scene 9 specifically. The obvious point the scene makes is that from Reader's perspective, Boswell made the wrong choice in becoming engaged to the splatterer. Reader desires him; she wanted him to choose her. Toward the end of act 2, scene 2, she cries out, "Oh. God. . . . Boswell. How long till you are mine?" (87). The conflict, however, is not in which woman he chooses; it is the subtler choice of engagement. To concentrate on his upcoming marriage to William and the attendant responsibilities such as preparing for the reunion with her children, the conceptual artist has put aside working on his new poster, even though he expected it to be "good." When Reader interjects that it would have been his "best" poster, his "signature," he agrees. "But still it's not that important," he goes on, because he needs assurance that by putting aside his engagement in creating a poster for his engagement in creating a marriage, he made the right choice. "No," she says. "You've made a mistake" (99–100).

Back in his apartment, Boswell returns his ward to the government and breaks his engagement to William, insisting that she has no claim to his affection because he never said he loved her. With her gone he returns to working on his poster as his "signature" (102): that which gives him his identity and his life significance. Once again love distracts from art as it did in act 1, but only after the action undoes a prior reversal. In act 1 love distracts from Boswell's efforts to ensure his legacy based on his Box Theory. Told he needs a beloved to change his insignificant life, he puts art aside because it distracts from his efforts to secure the marriage he needs before resuming his career creating posters. Told he made a mistake, and with his life ticking away, he puts love aside because it distracts from his efforts to establish a new basis for a legacy.

Boswell cannot simultaneously pursue engaging in love expressed in a relationship and engaging in imagination expressed in art. These competing claims on the self are incompatible in *Signature* as they are in *Abundance*. That is, *Signature* develops the conflict that *Abundance* introduces. The two protagonists feel the pressure of demands that would deplete that which they deem is essential to creating. Macon appeals to Bess as Max does to Boswell for financial help. Again, Macon, Max, and William appeal to Bess or Boswell for their time, asking that less time be spent on the artistic project, be it book, poster, or lecture tour. In Boswell's case, as Reader reminds him, it would be time spent on "children that are not even" his "own" (100). The three appeal to the two protagonists for a commitment of love—which empowers in Henley's plays of the 1980s—but that commitment would deplete the emotional energy the protagonists need for creating. Even if they wanted to respond—even if Bess did not feel betrayed and even if Boswell were not "shallow" (82), as Reader interprets his handwriting—they have limited resources for creating, depending on borrowed images. Boswell does not appropriate another's images as Bess initially appropriates Macon's, but he depends on the graphologist for the subject matter of the poster, which turns out to be a fiasco.

Answering an interviewer's question about the meaning of Boxdom, Henley replied, "Boxdom means a reduced way of thinking, in which you can put a box around anything. . . . If you make this truism big enough, it's a fear of the unknown, a fear of the mysterious and the spontaneous—it is what Boswell has."[11] His resources are limited because he never explores the unknown, the mysterious, the spontaneous within himself to release the contents of his unconscious, the images that the artist forges into art. In the play's closing scene, L-Tip tells William that therapy has made her aware of her unhappiness. In the same scene, after his poster has been destroyed and Reader admits she was insane and misled deluded clients, Boswell realizes he made a mistake and should have engaged himself to William, his beloved. But the play ends on that note. Of the twelve plays in the two-volume collected edition, *Signature* is the only one that does not end with a magical moment, the moment that issues from self-discovery.

The play has, in fact, a character who is creative: Reader.[12] The lone character not conceived naturalistically, she has a mustache and a beard, grows hair from her armpits that is long enough to braid and tie in a ribbon, and oozes blood, mud, and milk from her breasts. She is grotesque, but she does not lead Boswell astray. When he meets her, he is dying, has not created in years, directs his flagging energy toward stimulating public interest in a career that ended years earlier, and rejects William's love. Reader tries to make him aware of the irrational by putting him in touch with his deeper self because art is not philosophy. Creativity is releasing the unruly, irrational subsurface into the ruled, rational surface. "Look to the pickle," she tells him. "Take it into your heart. Sleep with it under your pillow. Walk with it in the dark" (87). That the public destroys Boswell's pickle poster reflects on his artistic skills and not on the public. That he cannot be in love while working on his masterpiece reflects on his level of emotional maturity and not on the graphologist's advice.

The critic might want to compare *Signature* and Shepard's *Angel City*. She or he should compare *Control Freaks* and Shepard's *Buried Child* for the insights into Henley's play that the comparison yields. Shepard's Pulitzer Prize–winning drama is set in an isolated farmhouse in corn-belt Illinois whose three inhabitants are an elderly couple, Dodge and Halie, and their middle-aged son Tilden, who enters the house in act 1 with his arms loaded with fresh ears of corn. When, in answer to Dodge's questions about where he got the corn, he says, "Picked it. . . . Right out in back,"[13] the father does not believe him because the land is barren; he has not planted in decades. When Tilden next enters the house, in act 2, his arms are loaded with carrots. In the interim two characters arrived: Vince, who claims to be Tilden's son, although no one in the house admits to recognizing him, and his girlfriend Shelly. To get through the unnerving experience, she sits on a stool at center stage, cuts ends off the carrots, scrapes them, and drops them into a pail.

Discussing the motivation of the characters in *Buried Child* and another Shepard family play, *Curse of the Starving Class*, Stephen J. Bottoms writes of their "need to belittle and control other inhabitants of the stage space by whatever are the most immediately convenient methods, so as to establish or reinforce a position in the family pecking order."[14] One example from *Buried Child* occurs at the close of act 2. When another son, Bradley, enters the house, he terrifies Shelly because Vince has gone to buy whiskey, Dodge is immobile on the floor, and Bradley's entrance, his wooden leg making his movements monster-like, causes Tilden to bolt from the room. Freezing, she obeys his command to open her mouth, at which time "*he puts his fingers into her mouth*" (107), keeping them there as he stares at her before removing his hand and smiling at her as the lights come down. For Bottoms, the act "has obvious overtones of rape and domination about it."[15]

A comparable scene occurs in Henley's *Control Freaks,* the set of which divides a residential property into kitchen, bedroom, and yard; in the yard is a "strange carrot garden."[16] Asked by her sister-in-law to pick some vegetables from the garden for the dinner salad, the woman, named Sister, follows her brother Carl into the yard where they argue about his wife's role in running the house. As the argument proceeds, she breaks the carrots she is picking in two and throws the pieces at him with the words, "Save the carrots! I'll cook them up for dinner and serve them with butter. I'll eat a big serving of them!" When Carl orders her to pick up the carrots she threw, she crawls on her knees. "I'm sorry" (127), she repeats Shelly's apology, "I'm sorry" (106), to Bradley for angering him after Tilden bolted. Like the amputee, Carl has his satisfaction. He jams a broken carrot into his sister's mouth and leaves her "*kneeling in the dirt*" (128). The image suggests fellatio, as does the scene in *Buried Child.* One assumes that Bottoms refers to the scene as an instance of the more generalized rape because there is no other instance of fellatio in Shepard's play. Yet there is in Henley's play, a blatant instance when Carl forces the play's fourth character, also crawling, to suck the poison antidote from a "*rubber cock*" (143).

The image is that of controlling another, but it is not the first image of control the play conveys. *Control Freaks* opens with Sister seated in the upstairs bedroom portion of the set speaking to the audience after serving on jury duty, a civic exercising of control in that she and the other jury members found the defendant guilty of violating cultural norms. Yet just as soon as the scene establishes an image of control, it is undercut with a counteracting image. In the downstairs kitchen, sister-in-law Betty rings a bell and calls, "Teatime!" provoking two responses from two selves of Sister's fragmented psyche of which she is unaware, selves that she does not control. Her Spaghetti self grumbles, "Fucking teatime," which the Pinkie self would placate with, "Be nice" (113). Not in control of herself, Sister is not in control of the property, even though her mother left the estate to her. Betty informs her that she and Carl were married while Sister was sequestered during jury duty; that she is in control is evidenced by her hanging a sampler on the wall and by her taking charge of Sister's pets. Yet as soon as the scene establishes Betty in control, Carl returns from work, and he in turn is in control because the culture is patriarchal.

At least the play's culture is patriarchal on the surface, for these early scenes dramatize a ruled surface covering an unruly subsurface that rebels against the rules. Betty prepares the daily ice-cream shake for her husband, the man of the house, who announces to Sister that he plans to start a furniture business, upsetting Sister, who wants to use the inheritance for a Frosty Shop. She defers to his plan, however, because he is her brother, though not without cajolements. To ensure that both his "girls" (117) are happy, Carl declares that since the man from whom he is purchasing the building wants to be a silent partner in the business, he will allow their votes to decide the issue. "Alright!" Sister says. "Well, then . . . whatever you think!" (118). Yet just as soon as he has checked one budding rebellion, another surfaces. Betty suggests that they find a man for his sister, putting him in the secondary role of having to agree or disagree with her initiative. He reclaims a little lost prestige by attaching a condition to the proposal, but Sister further erodes his power by reviewing her standards in men and how she will go about getting one. Despite seeking his approval, she has so usurped his position as sole arbiter of family values that he first scolds her for her language and then sends her into the yard to clean up the mess left, according to him, by a neighborhood dog but actually by him, for the audience later learns that he defecates in the yard.

If the opening and closing images of this sequence of verbal and visual images are excluded—Sister's fragmented selves reacting to the call for tea and her shoveling the mess into a garbage can—the mode of production is naturalistic and the interplay is a normal power struggle among three people, each with a claim to the property on which they live together. They are doing what the family members in *Buried Child* are doing in Bottoms' description: establishing or reinforcing positions in the family pecking order. With Sister out of the kitchen, however, the images become quirky. Henley has always mixed idiosyncratic images with more conventional ones. In *Crimes of the Heart,* Babe's revelation of her affair with a fifteen-year-old black youth is an example of a quirky verbal image. Bliss sitting on the commode or being with Frances as they remove their panties and throw them over the balcony are quirky visual images in *The Debutante Ball.* Sex has been present in *Control Freaks* with the two women vying for Carl's attention and, with the shake Betty prepares for him, his approbation. It is most blatant when the husband and wife "*kiss with a disgusting display of vile lust*" and Sister "*paces around them*" muttering, "Aren't you two a pair of lovebirds. Tweet, tweet, tweet!" (118). But alone the two lovebirds perform a ritual with Betty once again taking the initiative. Each day she wears panties with writing she sews on them that Carl has to identify. To assist him, she spins about the kitchen so that her skirt flares out while he drops to all fours, a position he maintains as he follows her spinning body into the bedroom. Based on Wednesday's writing, Lollipop Land, at least one day's act is cunnilingus. Her motivation remains the same: establishing or reinforcing a position in the family. Her strategy for achieving her goal can be compared with Sister's behavior.

Betty and Sister can be paired in that Betty is a ruled surface and Sister is an unruly subsurface with whom the former must deal because the latter has returned from jury duty, the mother left her the estate, and although Sister defers to her brother's business venture, she would prefer to put her money, which is more than he has, in another venture. Furthermore, now that she is talking about getting married and the two couples being "one big happy family," she and her prospective husband would own the controlling interest. As soon as she leaves the kitchen to shovel the mess, Betty asks Carl how soon he expects to "tell her to go" (118–19). The sister-in-law's strategy is to take possession of the estate with the business before Sister marries and to have Carl either nudge her out of the house or, if necessary, evict her. Her tactic is manipulating her husband with sex by arousing him, then controlling his arousal by dictating the act to be performed. Dropping to all fours, he not only becomes a panting Pavlovian dog following his mistress into the bedroom, he initiates a series of images that reveal his relationship with his sister, for just as the two women can be paired, he and his sister form a pair. And just as Betty orchestrates Carl's behavior, so does Henley orchestrate the interaction of the surface and the subsurface in a testimony to her ever-developing artistry.

Standing at her bedroom window, Sister freezes as Carl enters the kitchen below to sponge his face and neck, presumably after a vigorous bedroom performance. "It's him. He's down there," she says to herself; the actress should play the scene in a somnambulant state because she "*takes off her underpants*" and descends the stairs to wash them in the kitchen sink. Betty sews writing into her panties; Sister removes hers. Talking as she washes her panties, Carl confesses to a midlife crisis, concluding with the question, "Where's my roast beef?" to which Sister responds with a bowl of candies and a "Sure" to his asking her to feed them to him. With the brother eating the candies one by one until he is thoroughly aroused and, doglike, "*licking them out of the palm of her hand*" (120–21), this image fuses the scene's collective images, for it too is an image of cunnilingus. In this oneiric scene, is Sister struggling to assert control over her situation by controlling Carl's sexual responses as her sister-in-law does and, as the audience later learns, he did with her? Provocative, the image is ambiguous in a play that for one critic is "wildly comic," while another critic finds the characters "wholly evil."[17] Multivalent, Henley's theater yields multiple interpretations.

With the two together in the kitchen in the middle of the night and Sister's underpants in the sink, the scene is unambiguous to Betty, who has to get Sister out of the house and regain domination over Carl. When he suggests that Paul, the man from whom they are buying the building who is coming to dinner the next evening, the man on whom Sister has set her sights, take her off their hands, *Control Freaks* gives up the little resemblance it has to a naturalistic mode of production and instead relies on an internal logic dictated by the desire to control others. Henley specifies that the "set should be a frightening combination of dream real, fake real, and real" (112). The dream real becomes a nightmare. Betty relates to her husband an incident that occurred when they were checking the building they are buying from Paul for the furniture business. When Carl was in another part of the building, Paul proposed that she perform fellatio on him. Stunned, sickened, and finally enraged, Carl vows to kill him the following evening for the insult to her and the family honor.

The play has taken a hairpin turn. As her work evolves, Henley increasingly structures into her dramas action that veers from the set path or a mood or tone that clashes with the existing mood or tone. *Control Freaks* begins as a family drama but becomes a play noir, akin to the film noir, the ingredients of which are a femme fatale, sleazy characters, twisty plot, nocturnal scenes, and ominous atmosphere. By relating the incident to her husband, who vows to kill Paul after they sign the papers transferring ownership of the building, Betty ensures her triumph. With Paul dead, Sister will not have a man to marry and will therefore have to leave, while Betty and Carl will profit from sole ownership of the estate. Should something go wrong and Paul kill Carl, she will marry him instead, leaving her in control of a man described as a "sap" (122) and leaving Sister out in the cold. Her motivation is greed, her strategy is the manipulation of a weak man to do her bidding, her inducement is sex masquerading as love, and her goal is power: control of others.

Yet as soon as the genre of play noir is established, the action takes another hairpin turn. Having gotten Carl so worked up that he is committed to killing Paul, Betty has no reason to continue relating the incident; additional information about it serves no purpose. Yet she not only tells her husband that she performed fellatio on Paul—for his, Carl's, sake—she found Paul's semen not the "worst" of the "swallowed" (123) semen of men on whom she has performed this act. Also within this nightmarish scene are the playwright's trademark quirky images. Carl swears that hearing about the incident sickens him, but the stage directions have him "*secretly turned on*" (122). Since he is not sure whether he will kill Paul before or after dinner, Betty, who would like to know "for shopping purposes," decides to "cook in case" (123).

The play becomes a wholly evil, wildly comic postmodern parody of play noir until the next hairpin turn, which comes the following morning when Carl, called upon to settle a disagreement between the women, sides with his wife. Asked by Betty to pick vegetables for dinner, Sister follows her brother into the garden, where their quarrel ends with his jamming a carrot in her mouth, discussed above. In what is a pattern, he retaliates for Betty's controlling him by controlling Sister, visually with the carrot but also verbally by defending in the name of "rules" his siding with Betty in prohibiting the throwing of glitter after the ceremony of signing the papers with Paul: "Look, we have to have rules. Sometimes it's very good to have boundaries" (126). He joins a list of characters in Henley's theater who champion rules to counteract absurdity, thereby contributing to the absurdity. Neither is he aware of the irony in upholding the legitimacy of rules and boundaries after vowing to kill the dinner guest or the irony in his argument to Betty that if he does not avenge the insult, he will be shorn of dignity and "regress to all fours" (123), which is the position he regularly assumes with her, or the irony in his profession of "love" (121) to Sister. This irony leads into the second theme, according to Bottoms's analysis of *Buried Child*, that Henley's play shares with Shepard's play.

"The loss of any coherent connection with the past becomes an explicit issue" in *Buried Child,* Bottoms writes, "with the family's willful attempts to deny and distort memory through pacts of silence and blurred fantasizing."[18] That something happened in the past the characters confirm by their attempts to prevent its disclosure, but what happened is impossible to determine with certainty given the characters' conflicting versions of the drowning of a baby boy and the burial of the child in the backyard. With no onstage authoritative frame of reference, Shepard's play is a postmodern performance of autonomous narratives and perceptions, no one of which takes precedence over the others, so that the "past remains indefinable."[19]

Control Freaks has a coherent narrative in which the past becomes definable, but only by connecting the play's two sets of autonomous narratives. One set, which consists of the narratives of the three characters other than Sister, is more distortion than denial. Paul arrives early for dinner, picking up on his encounter with Betty when she and Carl were checking the building. When she tells him to leave, he reminds her of what she said about fellatio during their encounter, which is what she reported to Carl that he said: that she perform fellatio on him. At first she denies having said the words, then grudgingly concedes that she did, explaining her motivation as love for her husband. She is lying. Her motivation greed, she reported the encounter to incite Carl to eliminate Paul as competition for Sister's inheritance. Paul too is lying when he tells her that his motivation for warning her to stay away from the planned accident to the building is love for her. Not yet knowing that Sister inherited the estate, he wants to eliminate Carl. To woo her away from her husband, he attacks Carl with a revelation for which the play has no context. "He doesn't love you," Paul says to Betty. "He's too stupid to love you. He doesn't even know you were a whore and burnt apartment buildings for money and drowned your son in a bucket" (130). The revelation is that she drowned her baby son, the very crime that Dodge committed in *Buried Child*, assuming he really did kill and bury a child.

While Henley is mixing genres such as play noir and postmodern parody so that each one disintegrates as the prevailing genre, she is integrating repeated verbal and visual images across genres. The action picks up after Carl leaves Sister kneeling in the yard before crawling to the carrot basket, the scene that is followed by Paul's early arrival. The most frequent verbal image is mention of love, often occurring two or three times on a page. Learning that Sister inherited the property and is interested in him, Paul declares his "love" to her (134); learning that Betty wants Carl dead, he declares his "love" to her as well (139). When Paul first arrives, Betty declares her "love" for Carl (129); when Paul returns, she urges him to kill her husband. She even proposes a toast to "love throughout the ages" (141)—without mentioning the poison she added to the wine. In *Control Freaks* love is a mask for gaining control, the second verbal image. The poison Carl buys for the wine is "pest control" (131). "He just lost control" (136) is Sister's defense to Paul of her brother attacking him. When brother and sister leave the yard, Paul and Betty leap on each other but "*quickly try to regain control*" (138). The next time Carl confronts the guest, he assures him, "Everything's under control" (140), meaning that he will not attack again and that he will not have to because he added the pest control to the drink. The visual images of control are of one character having another kneel or crawl. Not every such instance is sexual—Sister kneels to collect the pieces of her broken gingerbread hors d'oeuvres—but when it is, it suggests cunnilingus or fellatio, and oral sex is not a loving act to please a partner but an image of domination and submission. Alone in the yard, Paul kneels before Betty; at her bedroom window, Sister looks down on her fiancé "*sucking on*" (140) her sister-in-law. For Paul to get the antidote for the poison, he must crawl to the pot Carl prepared and "*suck the potion off the rubber cock*" (143). The two verbal and two visual images combine in Carl's exulting to Sister: "I just liked seeing that slime crawl to me. It was nice. I had him under control" (144).

Connected, the first set of the three characters' autonomous narratives forms a coherent narrative of love's betrayal by distorting its power for the purpose of controlling others. The second set, Sister's interior monologues and sometimes dialogues that for consistency's sake can be called autonomous narratives, forms a coherent narrative that adds denial to distortion. When the two sets of narratives are connected, the past is definable, and in Henley's theater the past must be confronted—the true self must be discovered—for the present to change, creating the possibility of a new future. For the first time, Henley uses a stage image to display interiority, the state in which one discovers subjectivity. *Control Freaks* opens with Sister seated in her bedroom, a recessed space within the house where she lives with her brother. That she does not know herself is obvious from her ignorance of the two additional selves, Spaghetti and Pinkie, who exist within her. Any one or two or all three speak nine narratives. Examined individually, these narratives form a coherent tale of denial that connects with the distortion that surrounds them.

Since the actress playing Sister speaks the three voices, the audience does not realize that Sister is a fragmented self until the end of the first narrative, in the play's opening scene, when the actress adjusts her voice for Spaghetti's hostile reaction to Betty's ringing of the dinner bell for teatime and for Pinkie's attempt at conciliation. Even then, the audience would not necessarily suspect denial because the hostile reaction is understandable. Sister has returned from extended jury duty to find not only that her older brother has brought a woman into the house but that this woman has taken control of the house. Betty's presence would explain why Sister, presumably for the first time, has withdrawn into her inner life, her interiority. As she relates to the stranger in her house, Carl has been married before but always lived elsewhere with his wife before coming "back" to her and Mother. As soon as she says "Mother" (114), Betty expresses regret for the accident that killed her, the implication being that the accident was recent, so that prior to the time of the play, Sister was accustomed to seeing a familiar female face at home. With the mother dead and her brother having brought an unfamiliar wife into the house, Sister, thrust upon herself, releases facets of her psyche, her being, of which she is unaware, one of which is hostility toward the stranger taking control of the house whose preemption of the kitchen sends Sister into her bedroom. The jury duty also prepared her for dislocation from familiar territory. Sequestered with the other jury members, she was probably away from home for an extended period for the first time.

The only clue to the theme of denial in this first of nine narratives, but one gleaned only in hindsight, is in Sister's summary of the jury duty. The jurors put the defendant "away for good." Although she does not mention his transgression, and the fact that she does not may be a second clue, she is unequivocal about his moral deficiency: "He was a bad egg . . . a rotten apple . . . less than dirt" (113).

In the time that intervenes between the first and second narratives, Sister learns that Carl and Betty are married and that they plan to open a furniture business, a venture that requires her approval because the mother left the estate to her, and Carl, a salaried employee, lacks the capital to start a business on his own. Even before she speaks the second narrative, a discordant note is struck. When Betty turns on the machine to blend Carl's ice-cream shake, "*it makes a loud shrieking, monstrous sound that only Sister is aware of*" (117). Although the action does not need this detail, its inclusion contributes to Sister's developing character. Sensitive to the nuances of the relationships in the house, she alone senses the disharmony. Hence she turns inward, or in the stage design, she has an interiority that can be imaged. Before she explores that interiority, though, before she can trace the monstrous sound to its origin, the husband and wife discuss finding her a man, no simple task because making her desirable necessitates a "complete makeover," despite her claim that she "can look good" (119) when she wants to. Their denigrating remarks reinforce the self-deprecation she conceals under her exaggerated self-confidence. She leaves to shovel the mess the dog allegedly left in the yard while Carl drops to all fours to read the writing on Betty's panties as she spins around in the kitchen.

Spaghetti and Pinkie speak the second narrative while Sister sits motionless in her room and then walks to the window. Their wondering what to do is Sister's subconscious reaction to the new alignment in the family that Betty's presence creates, the business venture, and the degrading task assigned to her. Pinkie's remark at the window that she wishes she had wings to fly is Sister's subconscious desire to escape from the situation in which she finds herself. Invoking "Maw" (120) can be interpreted as a reference to a childhood wish for a Christmas present or a denial of the mother's recent accidental death, but it is not the denial that gives the narratives their coherence. Only at the end of this second narrative does she begin to approach the denial.

Standing at the window, Sister freezes at the sound of Carl's footsteps below, removes her panties, and enters the kitchen, explaining to her brother that although it is the middle of the night, she forgot to wash her "underwear" (120). The image of cunnilingus that follows—Sister's serving candy to her brother, who "*faster and faster*" (121) licks the candy out of her hand—can be interpreted as her subconscious desire to compete with her sister-in-law by controlling Carl's sexual responses. Another possible interpretation emerges: that Sister is subconsciously reenacting earlier scenes in her life that she consciously denies. Recognizing Carl's footsteps—"It's him" (120)—she removes her underwear and enters the kitchen, where she dutifully ministers to his needs after he bewails his misfortune in life. She leaves when Betty enters, to hang the underpants, which she washed in the sink, on the clothesline, but the play is not finished with the garment. That morning after Carl jams the carrot in her mouth, she checks the underpants, but they are too wet to wear. That evening, while giving her the antidote for the poison, Carl tells her to put them on because it is "not decent . . . to go around without anything on underneath" (144). She resists momentarily because they are still wet but then obeys. One assumption is that she wore all of her underwear except this pair during jury duty and has not yet washed the worn clothes so that this is the only pair available to her. She hangs the garment on a clothesline during a night succeeded by a Southern California "*pink-gold sunrise*" (124), and after a day in the sun, the garment is still wet!

The assumption is predicated on a naturalistic standard, that the sun's rays dry garments hanging on a clothesline. But the play is more nightmare than slice of life so that what Henley is doing is separating her heroine from the other three characters. All four act on two levels of reality, one of which is a level of deception. The difference between Sister and the other three is that whereas they are conscious of the deception, she is not. In the kitchen brother and sister declare their love for each other. Love for him is a mask for controlling—getting Sister to pledge her support, for example, in his achieving his goal of success in the business venture—for as soon as she leaves to hang the underpants, he and Betty discuss pawning her off on the sap invited to dinner. She wants to love him with the love a younger sibling has for a mentoring older one. Fragmented selves and images hint at another story, but she is unaware of them; her conscious mind denies them and the story. The deception is a self-deception, which is not the evil the others practice by consciously manipulating selves, making them victims. That she wants to love her brother, that she believes she should love him, is one reason, given the transgression, that she is fragmented. Yet since the denial cannot remain buried, the truth will come out by play's end.

Uncovering the denial begins in the third narrative. Hearing "*sounds of loud, violent lovemaking mixed with the sick sounds of deranged people*" (124), Sister awakens from a nightmare. Her conscious mind hears them as sounds made by Carl and Betty, whose "*disgusting display of vile lust*" (118) she witnessed in the kitchen earlier in the day, but they emanate from within her subconscious mind, which is beginning to impinge on her consciousness. "Where's my face?" she asks, feeling her identity in the house threatened by Betty's presence but also beginning to question who she really is. Smelling Carl's defecation in the yard, her Spaghetti and Pinkie selves argue about her history of "lying" her "whole heart out." In the second narrative, images hinted at another story. In this narrative, it is the allusions that do so. The first such is to *Hamlet.* Polonius's advice to Laertes before the son returns to Paris Spaghetti rejects. How can she "be true" to her "own self" if she does not know herself? The scene ends with a more telling allusion. Removing her wig, Sister reveals that she is "*nearly bald with horrible little bloody tufts sticking out all over her head*" (124). The description is that of Shepard's Dodge after Bradley gives him a haircut: "*His hair is cut extremely short and in places the scalp is cut and bleeding*" (83). The suggestion is that Henley's heroine has a buried past.

The fourth narrative, which follows the carrot-jamming scene, has the Spaghetti and Pinkie selves slapping Sister for her language that provoked her brother's action. Exhausted, she admits, "I don't know who I am anymore." Relief comes in the figures of her cats because even though Betty has caged them, she recognizes familiar forms to whom she can speak. Revived, she leaves the yard to make Carl "proud" (128) of her for getting herself a man in the person of the invited guest.

The resolution reveals Sister's state of mind. She does not rail against Carl for forcing the carrot on her. Instead, she blames herself for having "gotten lost" (128). She accepts responsibility for an unruly subsurface, a rebellious spirit, that labeled her brother a three-time loser in marriage and a "fucking failure" (127) in life. To accuse him of a transgression, however, would be premature, for the exploration of the darkness within has just begun, and she is still in the frame of mind that depends on his approbation for the sense of her worth. He is her mentor and guide, the person her culture has taught her to look up to, a person who can do no wrong, and that cultural indoctrination, when added to the psychology of a victim who blames herself for the crime, explains her self-deprecation. It is a culture in which the male has a distinctive identity but the female does not warrant one because she is mere sister to him. It is a culture in which the man does not hit the woman, not because he respects her humanity, but because she is a weaker vessel who has "woman problems" like "PMS disease" (138).

By intensifying pressure on the surface reality such as Carl's perception, Henley intensifies pressure on Sister's subsurface reality, creating the nine narratives that reveal both her self-deprecation and her struggle to throw off the yoke of the naturalistic perception and discover herself. In the fifth narrative, for example, addressing Sister's question about how to get a man, Spaghetti and Pinkie debate whether or not she is a virgin, leading her to express her "fear . . . of the unknown" (132). On the surface level, the fear is that of acknowledging she is a virgin or of losing her virginity. On the subsurface level, the fear is that of the interior journey because she does not know what she will discover about herself. Coaching Sister on how to play hard to get with Paul, Betty tells her that if she is too eager, he will discard her "like a piece of unfinished toast." Betty leaves, and in the sixth narrative, the Spaghetti voice within her says, "But I am less than toast" (133). An artist not afraid to take risks, as the sexual and scatological scenes demonstrate, Henley layers images with the different levels of reality to reveal different attitudes toward love. In the yard, Paul protests his love for Sister "more than words can say" while she experiences "*spontaneous orgasms*" (134–35). Believing him because she wants to believe she is worthy of love, she denies his duplicity until Carl, withholding the antidote from Paul, makes him confess that she is "nothing . . . but unfinished toast" (143).

The confession comes after the seventh narrative. At her bedroom window, she witnesses Paul "*sucking on Betty*" (146), a betrayal of love given their engagement, but she denies the betrayal, preferring to keep it a "secret" (142) so that she can die from the poison believing herself worthy of love. Yet once she confronts this betrayal, she can confront the original betrayal she has been denying since childhood in the eighth narrative, beginning in the voices of Spaghetti and Pinkie, "I'm thinking I'm remembering. . . . I buried it" (144). What she denied was Carl's sexual violation of her: a brother's controlling a kid sister in the name of showing her the "ropes" (145). The nightmare ends with Sister killing Carl as she repeats the words she spoke in the narrative that opens the play, the words that in hindsight provide the first clue to the transgression. The variation is in the shift from the third person to the second: "You're a bad egg . . . a rotten apple . . . less than dirt" (146).

Offering possible interpretations for the title of Shepard's play, Richard Gilman suggests an "image of the secret life of families, burying the issue of their lovelessness."[20] The suggestion works for Henley's play as well. The past is definable, for there really is a buried child: Sister. As a child, her self-worth was destroyed in the name of love. Her way of dealing with the outrage was to deny it, burying the violated child in her subconscious mind and thereby fracturing her psyche into a submissive young woman harboring a rebellious spirit. Her social development stunted, at play's opening she is torn between self-deprecation and brash self-assertiveness, between wanting to participate in life yet fearful of life given her childhood experience. To be whole, to integrate her fragmented selves, she has to confront the truth, thereby recovering the buried child in herself, freeing herself to love and be loved. Disinterring the buried child, she disinters love, for it too is buried.

Sister does not know of the existence of her Spaghetti and Pinkie selves throughout most of the play, but by sequestering herself in interior monologue and dialogue, she comes to know herself. In the ninth and final narrative, the closing scene, the three selves are united in liberation from the house of evil. As the figure flies over the audience in a harness lowered from the grid, Pinkie, the self that always wanted wings, spies Sister's dress on the ground, the dress she removed to put on the harness. "You remember Sister," Spaghetti says to Pinkie. "And now she knows. . . . Everything" (146). Despite Spaghetti's fear that they will die by returning, Pinkie insists, and the figure swoops down to grab the dress before flying away again. The play does not end with two selves abandoning the third self. The penultimate stage direction reads, "*She dances across the firmament with her dress*" (146). Disconnected from herself as a child, Sister has now found herself. Like *Crimes of the Heart*, *Control Freaks* is a drama of self-discovery that leads into a magical moment in which three selves, like the three sisters united as a family, are united in "one person."[21]

Sister's healing or integrating of herself is demonstration of the transition to healing or integrating the two engagements in Henley's theater: love in the plays of the 1980s, now recovered, and imagination in *The Miss Firecracker Contest* and the plays that open the 1990s. That desired reconciliation, the subject of the next three plays, is prefigured in the closing scene of *Control Freaks*. Flying is an image of, or metaphor for, the activated imagination, but if the imagination soars disconnected from a ground in reality, it becomes chimerical or, in extreme flights,

Icarian. At the least, the dreamer's human responses atrophy as in the examples of Bess and Boswell; at the worst, the dreamer is immoral as in the examples of Paul, Betty, and Carl. By returning for the dress, however, Sister's flying selves ground the imagination in love. Interacting and interpenetrating each other, the two engagements create a trilogy.

CHAPTER 4

1990s—A Trilogy of Experiments

What better place to attempt the reconciliation of love and imagination than the theater, for it is the nonpareil magical moment! And what better place for a communal, celebratory experience than the original theater! The title and structure of *Revelers,* the Henley play that makes this attempt, both invoke ancient theater, particularly comedy. As for the title, the term *comedy* is thought to be derived from the Greek word *komos,* which "means revel; there were several kinds of *komoi* and they took place on festivals, particularly of Dionysus, and consisted of or wound up with a procession of revelers, singing, dancing, and bantering the onlookers; there is a part of Aristophanic comedy which appears to represent a regularized form of *komos.*"[1] Structurally, *Revelers* opens with a prologue, the division of classical comedy and tragedy that gives the subject of the drama and the situation from which it develops, information the audience needs to know to follow the action.

Revelers is Henley's only play to employ a prologue. In it Victor, or Vickie, a film actress who began her career in Dash Grey's Red Lantern Theatre (RLT), makes a video in which she informs the others in the recently deceased founder's circle of associates and friends that although the memorial for Dash will be held at her northern Wisconsin cottage, her schedule prevents her from attending. The prologue serves two purposes. By supplying information about the event, it identifies the play's action as that of a ritual, and by supplying information about the actress, it identifies the ritual's counteraction. The ritual is the homage or worship due the founder of a theater; the opposing force is the satisfaction of a personal obligation. The action and counteraction constitute a conflict or incompatibility that is drama's matrix.

The prologue over, act 1 takes place in the living room of Vickie's cottage. The set further invokes not only ancient theater but also the god Dionysus, in whose honor the Athenian dramatic festivals were held in a theater consecrated to him on the slope of the Acropolis.[2] An "*ancient tree*" growing through the room gives the "*feel of enchantment.*" Various stage props —wig, veil, drums, "*hideous masks,*" and teddy bear—surround a "*life-size cutout replica*" of RLT's founder, Dash Grey. The description is that of a twentieth-century Dionysus. The "*sensual sneering lips*" suggest the god's dual nature, a god of ecstasy who can be a terrible god, while his "*gesturing triumphantly with a red umbrella*"[3] suggests the thyrsus with which the god is traditionally depicted. The color is that of red grapes, and the umbrella is a rod or staff the shaking of which opens the collapsed ribs so that their movement mimics the shaking of vines or leaves. The god of theater, masks, revelry, vegetation, and wine, Dionysus is the god of initiation.

Though the god's power is telestic, his contemporary counterpart's presence does not in effect an initiation in any of the circle in the first act, but the fault is not in the figure representing Dash. Though some of the circle profess to be the late founder's devotees, their power struggles, jealousies, and squabbles keep them focused on themselves. That is, the first act develops the play's initial counteraction of satisfying personal needs. With Dash dead and the RLT in financial crisis, its administrative assistant, Caroleena, is afraid that she will be let go. In an attempt to preserve her job, she directs Bob Gray in a video about his late brother. When Kate, a former acting student who left the theater to marry, enters the room, Caroleena says ostensibly to Bob but actually to Kate, "I'm in charge here" (152). When Kate refers to "our theatre," Caroleena questions her: "What theatre do you belong to, Kate Spoon?" (158–59). The administrative assistant has to be told that the housewife has invested in the RLT, helping to keep it solvent. With Caroleena out of the room, the housewife and Jasper, the RLT's artistic director, discuss terminating Caroleena's relationship with the theater. And with Kate out of the room, the assistant and Jasper discuss Kate's intrusion upon the memorial because she never belonged to the circle.

The men also contribute to the deflection of attention away from Dash and the figure representing him. Everyone agrees that Bob's monotone is deadly, yet when Jasper belittles Vickie's acting ability and Caroleena chimes in, he turns on his assistant for belittling a "very loyal friend" (156). Reacting to Caroleena's observation that the "circle" is complete except for Vickie and Earl Bell, the artistic director dismisses the latter as unworthy of an invitation; he was "Dash's minion of the month" (155). The first scene's surprise appearance is by Eddy Canary, a former writer and actor whose novel adapted for the stage made the RLT's reputation. He admits, however, that he came hoping to see Vickie.

As she does in all her plays, Henley brings together a collection of individuals who cling to the self-images and experiences that give them their identity. Caroleena begs Jasper not to let her go because she does not know what to do "without the Red Lantern Theatre" (156). Although Kate left acting school after Dash humiliated her for a classroom performance, she remains a hanger-on at the theater. To stay "afloat" while waiting to be acknowledged as a "world-class actor" (170), Jasper works in a fast-food restaurant, Chicken Bob's. Though she works in films playing Herlagator, a creature "with a tail" (155), Vickie believes she can return to the stage whence her career started. Though he has not written or acted in years and has become a derelict, Eddy hopes he and Vickie can start anew.

Clinging to their old identities, the characters feel they do not belong to anything other than those identities, with the irony that by clinging, they intensify their feelings of unbelonging and their formed selves. As a result, they are unhappy, lonely people locked in their self-absorption. Realizing she is being terminated, Caroleena pleads, "I can't live without the Red Lantern Theatre. Please. I can't live without it" (174). Cast aside by Dash after living together for fifteen years, embittered Jasper no longer finds "people attractive" (169). Kate does not expect Eddy to remember her because she is "no one he should know" (154); when they begin conversing, she refers to herself as a "nobody" (158). Eddy and Vickie were once lovers in an affair that ruined his marriage and ultimately killed his wife. Admitting to a "futile life," he sees himself as "no longer fit for human consumption" (169). Twice divorced with "no family, no friends, no children, no mate," she admits to being "miserable" (171). Even Bob, who is in the circle only because he is the late founder's brother and whose sole passion seems to be eating, is alone, his wife and children having left him for a man better able to express himself.

To overcome their low self-esteem, they seek to achieve recognition in either one of Henley's two engagements, love or imagination actualized as art, but pursuing the one puts a character in conflict with the second engagement. The entrance into the conflict is through the playwright's technique of pairing characters. When Dash humiliated Kate for her performance of a scene from Euripides' *Trojan Women,* she left the theater and married a man she "never loved" (154). Her reason for attending the memorial is to prove to the others, now that Dash is dead, that she has acting ability despite their lukewarm reception to her proposal to repeat the scene. "You assume I'm not artistic but I am," she says to Jasper; "In my heart I know I am" (159). Attending the memorial service by virtue of her financial support of the RLT, she is asked to show love—compassion for Caroleena—but she stiffens at Jasper's suggestion that the assistant be retained with reduced responsibilities, insisting she must be let go. "I'm afraid that's life" (157) is her callous indifference to Caroleena's situation, though not to Eddy's.

His reason for attending the memorial is to see Vickie, with whom he is still in love; his hope is that by reciprocating his love, Vickie will inspire him to create again, something he has not done since their falling out years earlier. Yet by attending the memorial, the one-time novelist is expected to be imaginative and write a poem for the service, a request that Kate makes of him. She even volunteers to be his "muse" (167), an offer he declines not only to avoid being alone with her but because any mention of his creative productivity since his one novel fills him "*with dread*" (158). Eddy is also paired with Vickie, but an examination of their drama is withheld until the examination of act 2. He does provoke a strong reaction in her. Claiming hatred as her emotion, she "*hurls herself*" at him (165) and has to be restrained by Jasper. The implication is that he left her to return to his wife, who subsequently died, at which time he began to drift.

Victor and Timothy Harold are a pair. She arrives in time for the memorial only because she thought it was the preceding week. Her reason for being at the cottage she owns is to get away from her role as Herlagator, in a cartoon created by filmmaker and cartoonist Timothy, following an accident in which she narrowly escaped being burned. She sees herself as imaginative, an actress who will one day return to the scene of her pre-Hollywood triumphs, as Lady Macbeth, for example, to play Blanche in *A Streetcar Named Desire,* yet act 1 ends with Eddy leading her out of the cottage and into the night, where he hopes to revive their old passion. Timothy, who is some twenty years younger than she and, despite his disclaimer that he is "too busy for love" (169), in love with her, follows her to the cottage to mollify her anger so that she will return to the filming. None of the others expects him to be imaginative, and he is not at the memorial. Where he is imaginative is in conversations on his cell phone with the filmmaking team, where he overcomes the objections to Victor's tantrum, for she is his "ideal vision" of Herlagator, as well as objections to her legs, for he can "animate" (167) them until they conform to the creature's dimensions.

The characters pursue their goal of achieving recognition in the identities to which they cling: their Apollonian selves, the opposition to which is the Dionysian dissolution. Since this opposition, one of many in *Revelers,* is particularly appropriate in a play that releases theater's original energy, it is best understood in these theatrical terms. Apollonian refers to the formed self, the actor in a characterization, whereas Dionysian refers to the process by which the actor becomes the character. For Charles Ludlam, founder of the Ridiculous Theatrical Company and an actor himself, the "Dionysian principle" is that "you're drawing on your own personality; you are committing an act of self-destruction, because you are obliterating your own identity to create another one."[4] In classical theater, Dionysian refers to the chorus in which individuals are subsumed under a group experience whereas Apollonian refers to the individual separated from the chorus to become an actor or character. But whether ancient or modern, the terms refer to interactive drives or energies with Dionysian a frenzied, chaotic flux generating the contents of the drama and the self and Apollonian a restrained, ordered dream fixing the form of the drama and the self.

Both are necessary for creativity. The Apollonian self needs Dionysian contents to form into dream, myth, art, self; while the Dionysian flux needs to dissolve the Apollonian harmony to allow for change and development into new forms, new harmonies. If generating contents is all there is to existence, then nothing is ever formed and life is purposeless and absurd, and if solidification of the contents is all there is, then generating ceases. The latter is what has happened to the above four characters: Vickie and Kate, Jasper and Eddy. So locked into themselves that they cannot engage in anything but their fixed self-perceptions, they are impervious to change.

The character who is imaginative in generating change is Caroleena, but not in act 1. In the first act, she claims her power is divinatory, an Apollonian claim, referencing Apollo's power as evidenced by his association with the Delphic oracle. In the second act, the audience learns she lied when she predicted Eddy's arrival. She chanced upon Eddy at some time before the memorial, and the two conspired to make it seem that she could foresee his arrival in the hope that if Jasper thought she possessed a special gift, the RLT would not terminate her. Her power as revealed in act 2 is empathetic and telestic, Dionysus's power as evidenced by his cult followers in Euripides' *Bacchae*.

Caroleena is also paired with Jasper in that she spurs him into accepting an emotion he thought dead in him, while he similarly prompts her into accepting an opportunity she thought dead to her. As the conversation ranges from the RLT's precarious financial state to Vickie's successes to Earl Bell's absence, the founder's rejected lover becomes more embittered until at the end of act 1 he says to the cut-out, "All for you, Mr. Grey. And what, what, what have you ever given me?" (174). Jasper exits to drink by himself, but just before turning on the cut-out, he says about Caroleena's exit that she is leaving "to kill herself" (174). She is not embittered about her love not being reciprocated despite confiding in Eddy toward the end of act 2 that she is "in love with someone who will never love" her. "It's a hopeless, doomed situation" (194), she pledges him to silence. The someone is Jasper, and the situation is hopeless because he is gay. The love is the play's one false note—and not because he is gay or ugly. In act 1, Jasper tells her to "stop having those feelings" (156) for him, as he has told her many times before, but what makes the feelings sound false is that she expresses them in conjunction with her pleading to keep her position in the theater. There is no desire in what she says; there is need. He is her supervisor. Yet Henley calls the administrative assistant's feelings love because the playwright needs to maintain the opposition of love and imagination.

Caroleena leaves the room at act 1's end not, as Jasper has said, to kill herself. The woman who introduces herself to Vickie as the RLT's "Jill of all trades" but with a "formidable acting gift" who hopes "someday to work on the stage" (161) has just learned she has been terminated. Yet even though a venue in which to actualize her imagination seems to be denied her, she leaves to obliterate her identity in order to create another identity: that of Dash-Dionysus. She leaves to transform herself, a power that makes her more Dionysian than Apollonian, for although both gods can transform themselves, it is a trait more characteristic of Dionysus because he is a slain and resurrected god whose followers partake of his power by imbibing him in wine, for example. Until she enacts her own transformation, Dionysus's presence is restricted to the cut-out, though Henley keeps the figure before the audience.

Act 1, scene 1 ends with the group moving to the property's Chinese pagoda for dinner. When the second scene opens inside the cottage, Eddy and Kate carry in the cut-out, which the group moved to the pagoda so that the late founder could be symbolically present at the dinner. As Jasper, learning of Vickie's arrival, enters, he points Dash's red umbrella at her while speaking to the figure of Dash as if he were alive: "She's come. Your protégé has returned" (163). During the scene Vickie's cartoonist colleague, Timothy, arrives to persuade her to continue in the role of Herlagator despite the accident when the creature exploded. He assures her he is having the "giant gator completely dismantled" (165). Timothy Harold represents everything that is foreign to Dionysus. A creator of mechanical creatures, he robs divinity of its theriomorphic potency. A technician who can animate Vickie's legs to fit the creature's design, he robs creation of its mystery, its sacredness. Jasper therefore has to identify the cut-out figure for Timothy: "Dash Grey. Great innovative genius of the Chicago theatre world" (165). The artistic director also ironically answers Vickie's question, foreign to Dionysus. Discomposed by Dash's death, Eddy's return, and the reptilian monster's explosion, Vickie wants a rational explanation: "Oh, what does it mean?" (165). Jasper's comments, spoken not in reply to her question but to keep her from attacking Eddy, invoke the nonrational nature of the Dionysian experience: "Dash wanted this to be celebratory. He asked us to revel in his honor" (166).

Act 2 is this revelry, although the stirrings are present in act 1. When Kate enters, crashing cymbals and rehearsing a passage in Euripides' play spoken by Priam's widow, she announces that the widow "Hecuba is resurrected" (172). Delivered as the one-time acting student gestures at the cut-out figure, the statement is ironic because by performing rites central to the cults of Dionysus and Dash, the members of the circle are resurrecting the god and the innovative genius of the Chicago theater world. For example, increasingly characters speak to the cut-out. After Jasper pours the champagne, he complains to "Mr. Grey" (174) that he is acting on his former associate's behalf without ever getting anything in return. The statement, however, is ironic for another reason. By performing rites central to Dionysus and Dash, rites central to theater, the members of the circle are performing the prerequisite for resurrecting themselves, for they are dead. Death pervades act 1. The flowers Vickie sent to the memorial are dead, as is the lizard Bob found in the pagoda. Eddy's face has a "*charming death grin*" (154). He cannot write; neither can Vickie respond to Timothy's appeal to their intimacy, brief though it was. Not only does she send him away, calling him a "fuckwit" (175), she refuses to drink the cheap champagne that Jasper takes with him as he exits the room to drink by himself, still embittered by Dash's ditching of him. To be reborn, though, they must imitate the god: be slain to be resurrected, be rent to be made whole.

Act 2 sets the stage for the death and rebirth by having the cut-out of Dash placed upon the structure erected so that each participant can perform before it a piece of his or her choosing to remember the man.[5] The RLT's founder comes to life in the person of Caroleena who, when it is her turn, appears with a red umbrella in a tree above the stage. Announcing, "I will be my dream" (184), she speaks a line that resonates in many permutations throughout this second and final act that consists of two scenes: a morning memorial service and an evening one.

To harbor a dream is to harbor a desire for a new self, a new Apollonian form. To realize the new self, one must actively pursue the dream. About her film career, Vickie says she "followed" her "dream" (187) until it was hers. Yet she also says she has "always dreamt of doing Blanche in *Streetcar*" (192), the realization of which would mean forgoing her film career, at least temporarily, to return to the RLT, a decision that would mean obliterating in the Dionysian dissolution her identity as Herlagator to create another one for Williams's play. Her actions belie her second dream. Confusing the date of the memorial, she arrives after the others. Because she has distanced herself geographically and emotionally from her former associates, she does not know of the theater's financial problems. She sleepwalks through her performance on the outdoor stage. Only after the morning revelry batters her Blanche dream does she finally admit in the second scene that the RLT is "just not relevant" (192). Not only is she returning to her formed California life, she intends to solidify it by marrying Timothy. These two leave before the evening memorial service takes place.

"Dreams aren't real" (179) to Timothy. His cell phone, laptop computer, and digital creations are real, as is Vickie, on whom he is dependent emotionally and sexually. When she dismisses him for "acting like a child," he admits, "I don't know how to act. I don't know how I should be" (175). A "cartoon cretin" (185), he is content with who he is, and he gets what he wants. Vickie agrees to marry him.

Kate has a dream, and for a moment she becomes her new self. Learning of the RLT's financial problems, Vickie vows to sell her West Coast estate, move back to Chicago, and "do the classics." Jasper is ecstatic: "Why, I can see you right now doing the Oresteia trilogy. Walking barefoot across a set of black steel." The image possessing her, Kate joins in: "Yes, I—I love Greek tragedy. I can never get enough. It's ancient, it's universal, the roles are meaty. Electra!" Seeing herself as Agamemnon's daughter, she is Electra. But since Jasper believes Vickie and therefore no longer needs the housewife's money to keep the RLT solvent, he throws an apple core at her as his judgment on the piece she performed as Hecuba in *Trojan Women,* repeating Dash's judgment in the acting class. Humiliated once again, Kate admits that people like her only because of her money, that she is "just an ugly, stupid woman filled with vain, pathetic, pathetic dreams!" (187–88). Lacking talent, she cannot realize her dream as an actress, and withdrawing financial support, she surrenders her dream of being involved in theater in another capacity.

As master of ceremonies, Jasper reads his former colleague's last wishes to the group. He introduces the different performances and performs with Vickie a number from his musical created for the RLT. And he too is possessed by his new self. Believing Vickie when she says she will relocate to Chicago, he sees himself not only running the RLT but running it in the image of his kind of theater: staging revivals of his musicals, for example, even though his musical version of Pearl Buck's *The Good Earth* was a "dead elephant" (186). But Vickie's decision to return to California shatters this dream because without her name to attract funding for RLT productions, and having alienated Kate, he cannot save the insolvent theater.

Eddy's dream has nothing to do with a theater career or the RLT's founder. Asked to write a commemorative poem, the best he can do is "Dash. I'm sorry you are dead" (184). His dream has everything to do with Vickie, whom he loves as he never could love his wife and about whom he dreamt the night before the memorial. "It was so clear I wrote it down," he tells her at the morning service. "It expressed things I did not know" (179). What it expresses is his feeling of inadequacy with her, for he is driven to her while being decapitated by her. Learning at the evening service of her decision to marry Timothy and return to California, he feels betrayed, yet he is incapable of acting with her. He says as much after showing her the dream that morning. To her declaration of love, he stammers, "It won't . . . No teeth" (190). The implication is that *work* is the missing word. Later she admits to Jasper that she intentionally shattered the dream by declaring her love, knowing that offering herself would "drive him away." For her, Eddy is a "sad, sad case" (192).

Dressed in a pink acrobat's costume, Caroleena "*falls, terribly ungracefully,*" from the wire running from a tree near the outdoor stage to a metal pole before climbing back into the tree and walking across the wire "*with agile expertise.*" Were she to stop at this point, she would be like the others: a performer doing her Apollonian piece. She does not come down. Aloft, "*transformed into the embodiment of Dash, taking on his voice and mannerisms*" (185), she so taunts and banters the others in accordance with Dash's last wishes to have the group "revel" (181) that she transforms a memorial to the RLT founder into a festival of Dionysus. And she does so by performing a new Apollonian self that realizes her dream of demonstrating a "formidable acting gift . . . someday . . . on the stage" (161). She is not completely absorbed by either role—at one point her "*Dash energy peters out*" before "*re-emerging*" (186)—but if she were, the opposing energy would cease to exert the counteraction necessary for creativity's interaction of generating and forming. As she is possessed, so she possesses the others. Although Timothy and Kate see her pretending to be Dash, Victor and Jasper are so caught up in the transformation, their consciousness is so altered, that they call her "Dash" (188), and she so acts her new self that an irate Jasper climbs the tree vowing to kill her. All of them are transformed from passive spectators of individual performances to active participants in a group ritual.

In act 2 of *Revelers,* Henley employs a new pair of images for the two forces or engagements that characters must interact if they want to make life as meaningful as it can be. The pair develops from the closing scene of *Control Freaks* where an self-integrated Sister swoops down from liberating flight to retrieve her dress. Flight is an image of the imagination, but it must be connected to a reality on the ground. In Henley's theater the ground is love, though her work recognizes other realities that ground dreams. History, collective and individual, and biology, for example, are determinants of identity. When in act 1 Kate takes the position that one is "never too old to make dreams come true," Caroleena disagrees: "And it's too late for you to be a prima ballerina or a concert pianist or the King of Norway or even a jockey" (173).

The play's most creative character, Caroleena, performs her Apollonian self above ground, directing her Dionysian transformation at those on the ground in a revelry that shatters their dreams of new Apollonian selves because they do not interact with a Dionysian ground. The first of two services, the revelry is not meant to destroy them, for she shows them that they can be creative despite the loss and suffering in that she performs the day after learning the RLT terminated her and she has no job to go to. Furthermore, she is in a "hopeless, doomed situation" (194) in that her love is unrequited. Yet she does not renounce love. It is her ground. She is "happy today" (194).

With one exception the others do not share her emotion. Vickie and Timothy do not attend the evening service because they feel no need to attend. They are not theater people; they are film people who return to filmmaking. Expressing her disappointment at having her dream shattered, Kate writes, "*Fuck you* in lipstick" (191) across the cut-out's face. Learning of Vickie's decision to marry Timothy, Eddy makes her "diabolical" (196) and her trademark insincerity. Saying "Let's just scatter these ashes and get the fuck out of here" (192), Jasper rounds up the others, referring to the ashes as "soot" (196). Thus the evening service begins as the morning service began with the attendees thinking of themselves and not of Dash, who despite a "troubled life" left a dying request for a "final celebration" (181). The first transformation slew their false dreams, dreams in which they could not realize themselves and which they scatter as they scatter the founder's ashes in accordance with his wishes. They are to celebrate too, but they cannot until they connect themselves to the scattering as an experience that subsumes their individual suffering.

Though he is not in costume and does not appear above them in a tree, Bob's performance effects the second transformation. His question at the end of the morning service, "When do I do my piece?" (189), surprises, for his video interview in the opening scene is so emotionally neutral that he would seem to have no interest in performing, an interpretation he supports by stating that he never saw any of the plays his brother staged when they were growing up. Yet he so wants to perform that he requests time at the evening service, prefacing his recitation with the admission that he secretly watched the play from which the excerpt is taken "over and over again" when he and Dash "were little" (197). Theater enthralled him, but he denied the fascination and his brother's achievement by denying any knowledge of the theater or Dash's work, even maintaining a different spelling of his surname than that of his brother, until he is onstage with his fists clenching the ashes. He becomes his brother, reciting the latter's lyrics that invite the spectator to "run . . . dance . . . play and sing," festive experiences that the late founder's testament beseeches the circle to enjoy at the celebration. An experience not urged in the testament but appropriate to the memorial is in the repeated line, "Cry if you must" (197). By imitating Dash at the morning service, Caroleena brought to life the theater founder and figure of the reveling Dionysus. By imitating him at the evening service, Bob brings to life the theater founder and figure of the suffering Dionysus. Hearing the line, Kate, who took no ashes because Dash denied her talent, cries, and just as suddenly, the scene is transformed into a magical moment.

The classical scholar E. R. Dodds is an authority on Dionysian possession, calling it the "merging of the individual consciousness in a group consciousness." The cult worshipper "is at one not only with the Master of Life but with his fellow-worshippers; and he is at one also with life of earth."[6] In this scene in *Revelers,* Apollonian selfhood is transformed in Dionysian dissolution as individual emotions merge in a group experience. The five connect as they have not until this moment. Kate encourages those who feel like crying to cry. Feeling the ashes drift through his fingers, a pensive Eddy remarks on life's insubstantiality—"Strange how little we weigh" (197)—and a contrite Jasper regrets not having saved ashes for Earl Bell, the lover for whom Dash ended their relationship. Bob, who held onto his while reciting, gives them to Jasper.

With the ashes on the ground, Bob calls everyone's attention to the "changing . . . colors up there." Looking skyward, Jasper says, "Yes, I know. Such a sunset. Dash's last" (198). They accept death, but it is his last sunset and not theirs because they are still alive and, appreciating such a sunset, can celebrate life despite their shattered dreams. Or rather because of them. Eddy feels "bones . . . bits of them" (198) in the ashes. Feeling the fragments of the life that was Dash's drifting to the ground, he feels the mystery of death in life: the death, for example, of his dream of a life with Vickie. Reconciled with death, he and Jasper and the others can reconcile with life. They can feel the mystery of life in death: the generating of new dreams.

A Henleyan heroine, Caroleena exemplifies the drama. At play's opening she is fearful of losing her job, unsure of herself in coaching Bob in the video, and resentful of Kate's presence at the memorial. Anxious to prove herself to the other members of the circle, she conspired with Eddy to trick them into thinking she had psychic powers. She does impress the others, but not by trickery. She impresses them by donning a safety harness, climbing into the tree, and imitating Dash. Discovering herself by drawing upon the depths of her interiority and actualizing the interiority in the makeshift theater, she proves her worth to herself as well as to the others. Liberated, she can add the sound "Poof" (194) to her revelation to Eddy that the plan she concocted with him did not save her job, and she repeats the sound until the play's last line elevates it to a refrain. In context, "Poof" suggests the impermanence of plans, dreams, and Apollonian selfhood, for life's opposing force is Dionysian dissolution of selfhood. She went from self-deprecation to self-realization at the cottage, but knowing she cannot stay at the cottage, she negotiates a ride back to Chicago with Kate, giving Eddy the idea to also ask for a ride. She "*flings her ashes with a magical quality, as though they were fairy dust*" (197) until they are gone, at which time she pretends "*to sling more ashes*" (198), not in disrespect but because she knows that all dreams become fragments to be strewn so that the particles can be rebuilt into new dreams—new life—as Dionysus, god of nature, is slain to be resurrected. In the play's closing scene, Caroleena and Bob, who accepted an offer from Timothy to go to Hollywood, lead the others in a magical moment that is a scene of self-discovery for the others. Accepting the death of Dash and their dreams, the five can now accept change. And accepting change, they celebrate death's transformation, imaged in a handful of ashes and a changing sunset, into life's renewal.

In this moment the celebrants reconcile Henley's two recurring engagements: love and imagination. As they experience the bond of love in mourning, the sunset at which they are looking "*deepens to a multitude of unbearable, beautiful colors*" (198), the last two words recalling the colors flooding Carnelle's face at the fireworks display and Bess's description of the rivers she saw during her missing five years. *The Miss Firecracker Contest* and *Abundance* explore the discovery of imagination in a theater in which love is the discovery. *Control Freaks* and *Revelers* momentarily reconcile the two discoveries. The first play reconciles in one character the two discoveries or engagements that have competing claims on the self; the second reconciles in a group the two engagements. The task the playwright faces at this juncture is finding a form in which to reconcile them.

Henley makes her task more challenging by returning to the past, but this return is necessary because the future becomes new only by returning to the past, as the figure in the harness in *Control Freaks* goes back for Sister's dress and the figure in the harness in *Revelers* goes back to the time when the circle members formed their dreams. In addition to returning to theater's origin, *Revelers,* the initial play in what can be considered a trilogy, combines the two sets of fragments Henley has always combined: those of her characters' divided psyches and those of absurd contemporary life. To these fragments she adds in the trilogy's next play disconnections on a scale unlike those of the preceding plays.

In the introduction to *L-Play,* she writes that she "had several notebooks with interesting bits of dialogue, evocative images, compelling settings, and so forth." But since "nothing was jelling," she became "distraught" until, realizing she was "fragmented, decentralized, clueless," she got the "idea for the play," which was to take the notebook entries and make them the material from which to write a "variety of different scenes in different styles and different characters" from the "mosaic of life." That is, the rewritten entries would remain fragments whose "only unifying element would be that the title of each scene would begin with an L" (xii). Her statement in the general introduction that precedes the individual introductions seems to support her perception of the play. Its "central theme is: Nothing is central, all is fragmented and a mess because there are just too many styles, times, characters, and chaos to choose from" (vii).

The difficulty with the perception is that a study of *L-Play* uncovers a design to the scenes, a contradiction the playwright herself recognizes when, after making the point that each scene's title begins with an L, she concludes with these two statements: "An L is half a box. It is a letter that is searching to connect, to link" (xii). The search will discover patterns that yield a design that connects the fragments into a quest that forms a coherent play and theater.

L-Play consists of twelve scenes. The first, titled "Loneliness," is set in a Louisiana diner. It opens with a waitress speaking on the phone with her daughter and then her mother, with whom the child has been living for some time, presumably since the speaker was sentenced to prison. Although she assures the girl that she will be invited to her wedding to the diner owner, she disabuses her of the expectation of living with them. "Maybe you could visit us some . . . I said maybe."[7] The phone conversation over, a teenage girl enters and identifies herself as the diner owner's granddaughter about whom Monica, the waitress, has heard because the girl was in some kind of trouble. A man enters the diner. After placing an order, he accuses Monica of having caused the suicide of a senator for whose political campaign the two had worked in the past. Taking out a gun, he shoots and kills her. Before he leaves, though, he tells the teenager to "shake her" to make sure "she's dead" (206).

In the second scene, "Linked," in a Los Angeles apartment, a woman is helping a man compose a letter to the woman who threw him out. Whether the latter woman is his wife or his girlfriend is not stated. Neither is the past relationship of the two in the apartment stated, although from the conversation it is apparent they were linked in the past and remain friends in the present. So too are the scenes linked. Before the man can send the letter, he will have to recopy it because it has "bloodstains" on it (207), which picks up the image that closes the first scene. Echoing the first scene's title, the woman says she is "lonely"; "No, really, shoot me if I ever . . ." (208), she interrupts recounting an instance of her blighted love life. The scene opens with her exasperation with a neighbor's hacking cough. At one point she yells out the window her wish that the neighbor "would die" (207), and the scene closes with her complaint that "she's still alive" (210).

These first scenes are also linked in another way. Set in a South Louisiana diner with no customers until the teenager and then the man enter and in a cheap Los Angeles apartment, the time of each nocturnal and the atmosphere sordid, they are naturalistic slices of life with characters caught in forces over which they have little control or understanding. Yet the mode of production is not naturalistic. Henley experiments with sound and lighting to set a scene so that what the audience sees is not representational, but suggestive. And not every scene is a naturalistic slice of life. The illogicality of dreams infuses the third scene, "Loser." A man, Malcolm, is overjoyed to be invited to a party, interpreting the invitation as a sign that he has been professionally and socially accepted. Once there, however, he learns that he is being fired and that the host, his employer, invited him only to entertain the guests, which he does by "*making flatulent sounds from underneath his armpits*" (214). The bizarre aural and visual images, for he is nearly naked while performing, do not negate the verbal linkage, which strengthens from scene to scene. When in the first scene the waitress admits she is sorry for what happened to the senator, the man threatening her with the gun seems to relax, saying, "You have to tell people what they want to hear or they don't come back" (206), but he shoots her anyway. With slight modification, the host repeats the line as advice for Malcolm if he wants to get on in the world.

The repeated images form patterns of linkage that begin to sketch in a design, which is the progressive disconnection from the web of relationships that bond people. The design begins with the rejection of family, nuclear and extended: Monica's rejection of her daughter and the teenager who comes to the diner looking for her grandfather, the owner Monica expects to marry. In scene 2 the woman curses her neighbor. In scene 3 the party guests, who represent society, perceive Malcolm as an object of derision. The consequence to the individual is a disintegrating sense of self-worth, with the attendant emptiness filled by a feeling of self-deprecation. The consequence to society is a disintegrating sense of community, with the vacuum filled by the fragments of absurd contemporary life.

Another consequence to the individual is alienation not only from others but from the self. Malcolm is a loser because he accepts the naturalistic perception of him as a fool; he is therefore alienated from his true self, as is the Lunatic, the subject of scene 4, which opens with a variation on Henley's rejected-child motif. The speaker explains that she does not want children because childbearing makes a woman fat and the change in her figure might result in her loss of self-esteem and dependence on a husband "to be supportive" (215). She continues the unraveling of the web of relationships that bond people because, although described as a "*frumpy housewife*" (215), she apparently lives alone and does not want to be dependent on anyone.

The form of scene 4 is a gauge of the distance its subject has extended the earlier disconnection. Scene 3 is a dream sequence in which Malcolm encounters various characters. Though one actor plays all these other roles, Malcolm interacts with them; he engages in dialogue with them. Alone onstage for her scene, the Lunatic delivers a monologue. Without interaction with others, her world is a further disintegration of the sense of community, the consequence of which is that she is totally dependent on her self, even if it is only a physical self, for her identity. Thus when she experiences light-headedness brought on by a lack of nourishment in her fat-free diet, she causes an accident in a supermarket and slips in and out of consciousness, the sole images of which are of "chilling incidences," one of which she relates. In a mad dream, she awoke in bed with a man or a woman, she was wearing roller skates in the bed that had fruit all over it, and she had a banana that she conjectures had been partly eaten "up [her] 'vagina'" (216). Losing her sanity, which connects the self to a ground in reality, she loses her self and becomes a lunatic.

Scene 5 introduces the design's counteraction that transforms *L-Play* from a collection of scattering fragments into a drama. Its subject is the Learner, who is both similar to and different from the subjects of the two preceding scenes. The Lunatic's fat-free diet leaves her light-headed. But it is the soul's engagement that leaves the Learner, a "*pale, emaciated*" (216) college student, light-headed, for he has fallen in love with a classmate in a poetry course. Conscious of the image his shabby clothes give him, Malcolm declines the butler's offer to remove his coat, removing it only when he accepts the host's perception of him as a fool. So too is the Learner self-conscious as he tries to imagine how his classmate perceives him: "Did she suspect that I have trouble reading the longer books? Holding them up with my frail wrists, reading the tiny print with my bad eyes" (217). He, however, does not allow himself to be reduced naturalistically, nor does he reduce her naturalistically, though she was a candidate for such a perception with her body encased in a back brace and a "pale" face that turned "terribly red" and "blotchy" (216–17) when she cried. Her condition enabled him to overcome his timidity by carrying her books until her brace was removed. Undeterred when she now declines his offer of assistance, because he was smitten when she wore it and in love with her after it was removed, he sees past her physical self while considering the likelihood that she cannot see past his frail wrists and weak eyes.

The form of the Learner's scene, a monologue, is similar to the form of the Lunatic's scene, yet different too. She talks only about herself, her diet, her bad dream. He talks about himself and his feelings, but his feelings are directed toward his classmate. He is the scene's subject, but she is his subject in imagery that connects with imagery inside and outside the play. He opens his monologue by expressing his dislike of T. S. Eliot's poetry because he does not understand it, though he is not averse to appropriating images from it. Afraid to speak to his classmate when first attracted to her, he identifies with the protagonist of Eliot's "The Love Song of J. Alfred Prufrock" by characterizing his shyness as "afraid to eat the peach" (216), an image from Prufrock's contemplation of his emotionally constricted future—"Do I dare to eat a peach?"[8]—and an image that connects his story with the Lunatic's story of awakening with "fruit all over the bed" (216). Eliot's poetry also connects *Revelers* to *L-Play,* for Jasper quotes the opening line of *The Waste Land* (157) in the earlier play.

Repeating images with minute variations is Henley's principal technique for connecting all of the play's stories into one story. Light imagery is crucial to *L-Play.* It is introduced in the second scene when the woman helping to compose the letter criticizes the woman to whom it is addressed: "That she didn't know the difference between ephemeral and diaphanous. Or she mistook opaque for translucent?!" (209) "*Fractured light scatters, swirls across the stage*" (211) for the setting of Malcolm's scene; the "*blue screen*" of the television "*flicker*[*s*]" (215) in the

Lunatic's scene. In the Learner's monologue, light focuses on the classmate, whose name is Lucheea, the root of which is *lux,* the Latin for light.

The Learner sets out to write a poem inspired by her. "My coy one! Lucheea!" (217), he rhapsodizes. "My coy one" invokes Andrew Marvell's "To His Coy Mistress," a poem that connects with the "'Proofrock' poem" (216).[9] The Learner is no speaker of a seventeenth-century poem, nor a twentieth-century poem. One reason is that he has yet to complete the poem inspired by Lucheea. He will in a later scene, for he and the Lunatic are the play's two characters who appear in more than one scene. Relating her bad dream, she tells of the banana "up [her] 'vagina'" Since she follows the word with the clause, "as they call it on the six o'clock news" (216), she is aware of another word for that part of her anatomy, just as she is aware that she is addressing the audience. Lacking her sensitivity and not addressing the audience, one of the two men in scene 6, titled "Lost," verbalizes the word.

At a bar in a pool hall, two men, who could be brothers, are discussing the change in color an orgasm effects in a vagina, except that they also use the crude word "cunt." The older, Ben, who knows from having watched the change in his girlfriend's, Shelly's, "cunt," advises the younger, Wes, to light a match or shine a light if the room is dark when he is in bed with a woman so that he can see for himself. He even recommends Shelly for the experiment. Wes disagrees because he does not think that she is interested in him, but Ben assures him that if he "spend[s] money on her, she'll come right around" (218). Though love is not in their emotional experiences, at least Ben understands the ritual of courtship. Shelly is not his girlfriend, he protests; she is simply the woman he "fucked for trinkets," but he understands the function of the trinkets. The cretin Wes cannot understand why he has to buy her anything. "I mean," he says, "she's not buying me presents" (219). Nevertheless he grudgingly agrees and, with the five dollars Ben gives him, leaves to buy Shelly a present.

As he finishes his beer before leaving, Ben is described as "*very lost*" (220). According to him, women are pushovers for affection "because their fathers never loved them. Or maybe nobody ever loved them. But their fathers didn't for sure" (219). Since he reduces women to a naturalistic explanation, be it psychological or biological—since he cannot perceive a spiritual nature in them—he is a typically lost Henleyan male character. But why is Shelly, who comes to the pool hall looking for him, also described as lost? She cannot be faulted for missing the irony in her explanation to Wes that the beauty mark he admires on her neck is really a mole that she will have "checked for cancer if it changes colors," for she was not privy to the earlier conversation about her anatomy changing colors. She can, however, be faulted for not seeing through Wes's stratagem of suddenly appearing before her with a "*dime-store bottle of cologne*" (221) and an offer of a beer. Starved for attention after angering Ben on a recent date, she chooses not to see, so that the scene ends with her sitting "*lost and nervous*" while Wes buys the beers until she looks at the cologne and her face "*glows*" (222).

Scene 6 is the light imagery's nadir. Shelly's glowing face prefigures another change in color in her anatomy, but without her emotional engagement the act causing the change is but another fragmented experience such as the ones the first few scenes dramatize. And although the orgasm satisfies, the experience lacks the qualities that distinguish the lover's appeal in "To His Coy Mistress." Had the lover and his lady "world enough, and time," he, for example, would devote a hundred years to praising her eyes, for she "deserve[s] this state" of adoration. Since they do not have unlimited time, with their hearts and bodies engaged, they can make the most of the time they have, taking their pleasures "thorough the iron grates of life."[10] For Ben, life is much simpler and more easily penetrated. Dispensing with figures of speech, he advises Wes, "If you want to get laid," buy the woman a "fucking trinket" (219). Lacking the seventeenth-century lover's imagination and the Learner's love, he demystifies life.

Scene 6 completes the first half of the play's design; scene 7 commences the search for the patterns that complete the play's overall design, with new light imagery, self-discovery that leads to a magical moment, and a connection of imagination and love.

Scene 7, "Lunatic, Part II," is the Lunatic's second appearance. In a monologue delivered in an asylum, a lucid Lunatic tells what she must do to be "set free to leave" (223) the asylum—set free from her disordered state. She has a recreation-room "puzzle to solve," a task that requires assembling its pieces—"fragments, shards" (222). She knows she is responsible for the task and therefore cannot blame a force or agency over which she has no control; in her effort to frustrate the recovery process, she has been mixing into her puzzle pieces from other puzzles as well as so ruining individual pieces that they must be discarded. A second task, already begun, that she does not indicate also is an implicit prerequisite for being set free: assembling the pieces of a second puzzle, this one within her memory. Her first monologue closed with her unable to remember many details of her life between her adoption of a fat-free diet and the bad dream she had. The second monologue opens with her talking about the meals she must eat on a daily basis as part of her therapy.

The fact that she relates her disordered state to the deficiency in the fat-free diet and her health to a more balanced diet connects her present condition to her past behavior. Recovering her past, she is recovering from her disordered state.

Scene 8, "Leaving," dramatizes the consequences of discontinuity between the past and present. The mode of production "*should be . . . stylized,*" with two women, wearing symbolic half-masks, positioned next to each other. The grandmother has a tradition, for her mask is "*ancient,*" but since she does not transmit the tradition, the mask is "*decadent, and decayed.*" Without a heritage, her granddaughter wears a mask that is "*defiantly neutral*" (223).

To fill the emptiness in her life, the granddaughter begs her grandmother to tell her about the lover she had, an experience that she promised to relate one day. The older woman either ignores the request or says that she has "forgotten that story," even though the granddaughter places the liaison in the summer the grandmother cut off her hand. Her other answers reveal an addled mind. All that she can remember about her son, her granddaughter's father, is that he "didn't take care of his teeth" (224). The one subject in which the older woman shows an interest, and of which she has knowledge, is her jewelry. She remembers she put rings on the fingers of the severed hand, and she knows she owns jewelry because she asks her granddaughter to fetch the case so that she can wear a necklace and a bracelet. Yet other than a red balloon she has left the younger woman as a "remembrance" (225), the grandmother has nothing to give her—no heritage to transmit. The granddaughter is left with nothing, not even a filled balloon. As the older woman dies, the air "*rushes*" (226) from the remembrance, leaving a shriveled balloon in the younger woman's hand.

In his second monologue, in scene 9, the Learner, like the Lunatic, connects with his past by remembering wearing galoshes in fifth grade, though he makes the connection as he speaks anything that comes to mind in an exercise to keep the mind open for an idea or image to surface. He does the exercise because he wants to write a poem to Lucheea, but he does not know how to begin and "nothing flows forth" until, listening to the sound of L repeated, he connects with a heritage. He opens a dictionary, the repository of verbal images in English formed through the ages. As he reads the L-entries, he gets an "idea": he will write an L-poem for Lucheea featuring the word "love." Since it is not in the list he reads, it must flow from his feeling for her. His imagination stimulated, the monologue ends with his repeating, though not with absolute fidelity, the titles of the scenes of *L-Play,* inserting the one word that is not the title of a scene but contains the letters missing from the play's title: love. And he inserts the word in such an order as to imply it is in opposition to the title of scene 6, the pool-hall scene, so that the monologue ends with "lost, love, life. . ." (227).

Scene 10, "Life," picks up as its title the last word of the Learner's monologue. It revisits the image of Malcolm's funny shoes in "Loser" because one of the scene's forms is imaged as a shoe. It picks up the image of nothingness that ends "Leaving," with the granddaughter holding a shriveled balloon, because its opening presents life before there is a magical moment or a community or a heritage to transmit. Life's first rituals the scene performs in pantomime after Shoe's arrival. Before this arrival, three mud-covered forms, identified as Big One, Middle One, and Small One, emerge from holes. An amplified offstage voice that narrates the scene comments on their "*dazed and stupefied*" condition: "They never celebrated occasions and failed to share or savor the moment" (228).

Shoe's arrival marks the beginning of consciousness, behavior, and rituals. Feeling threatened by the strange phenomenon, the Ones react "with menace," imprisoning Shoe. Their behavior becomes the first of two rituals. Big One "*acts out*" Shoe's "*butchery,*" provoking a "*dance of blood lust*" that "*builds to animalistic debauchery*" (228). Only the Ones' need for sleep prevents them from proceeding.

During the night Small One comes out of its hole and begins to interact with Shoe, cruelly at first but gradually responding to Shoe's kisses until they are "*laughing themselves sick.*" Their behavior initiates the second ritual. Awakened by the noise, Middle One emerges to send Small One scampering and to order Shoe back into the cage. Yet as the latter "*dances elegantly,*" Middle One comes under the spell, and the two join "*in the enchanted dance.*" Accompanied by a "*burst of red stars*" exploding across the sky, the dance becomes a magical moment. This ritual is the antithesis of the first ritual, for although Middle One danced the blood-lust ritual, the narrator says about the second dance that "never having danced, it was a great occasion for the Middle One who fell in love with Shoe and wanted to save it from all harm forever" (229). With dawn's advent and Big One's stirring, the two flee. So too do the remaining Ones exit, Big One carrying Small One, whom it brutally beat to vent its frustration upon discovering the flight of the prisoner and Middle One.

In *L-Play,* Henley traces the loss of love in the pool-hall scene, for example, to humankind's origin and its two choices, the dance-ritual of life or the dance-ritual of death. In a hairpin turn typical of the playwright's dramaturgy, Shoe and Middle One return, their love reduced to lust and consequently spent. In images evocative of Beckett's two tramps in *Waiting for Godot,* Shoe and Middle One halfheartedly attract and repel, shrug off and gesture to each other until they part, only to return to stay "*together but apart*" and with "*untold anguish*" for their loss.[11] Their situation cannot be maintained, however. First comes Small One's return followed by Big One's return—savagery's return. While Small One and Middle One watch, the latter powerless to stop death's fury, Big One dismembers Shoe, and the three "*eat the victuals, blood dripping from their mouths*" (231).

These hairpin turns are presented visually, but the scene ends with a verbal reversal. "They knew they had been through something" (231), intones the narrator. The "something" recalls the "something" (226) the granddaughter begs for but does not receive from her grandmother in scene 8. The Ones have a blood-lust ritual, a dance of death, to transmit to their progeny, but they have something else that they did receive. They have Small One's frolics with Shoe and Middle One's love for Shoe, whose arrival is described as a "gift" to "primitive beings" (228). Unlike Wes's pool-hall "gift" (221) of cheap cologne, love is a gift of the heart, but the recipient must work at keeping it vital, for it can be ignored, rejected, betrayed. Yet it can also be renewed. Dismembered, it also renders life whole, creating a magical moment, the blueprint for a community, a body of people cultivating common practices and beliefs into transmittable traditions. Thus the play's two remaining scenes actualize the quest for love and the human values it undergirds.

Recalling images from earlier scenes, scenes 11 and 12 confirm the twelve scenes' continuity. Scene 11, "Lunatic, Part III," again belongs to the Lunatic. Her "*tattered circus dress*" recalls Malcolm's fool's outfit in the "Loser" scene. The "*net skirt*" recalls the web in which the Ones imprisoned Shoe, while her missing leg recalls Shoe's dismemberment. Her awareness that "no other performers" are onstage "to share the finale with"

(232) recalls both the title of scene 1, "Loneliness," and the woman's complaint in scene 2 that she is "so lonely" (208). The invitations she says she must send for the party she considers giving recall both the party invitation Malcolm accepts and the party invitations the grandmother's guests decline in the "Leaving" scene. But scene 11 does not simply recall for continuity's sake. It gathers up the earlier images into a design that defines the play's coherence. In her previous monologue, the Lunatic admitted that she knew she had to solve the puzzle to be released from the asylum. She must have solved it because she is free, if not yet from the asylum, then from the disordered state that had made her a patient.

She connects with her past, acknowledging the supermarket accident and the bad dream brought on by the fat-free diet. She connects with her present as well, acknowledging that her attempt to "hack . . . off with garden clippers" her missing leg led to complications and amputation. She connects with herself not only by learning how to walk on one leg aided by crutches but also by acknowledging long-repressed feelings about loneliness. In a Dantean image, she feels she is "circling the pit. A final walk on the rim" is in store if she continues her downward spiral away from human contact. In a Henleyan image that figures in characters' self-discoveries in the plays of the 1980s but disappears for a time in the 1990s, she muses upon the freedom that being alone ensures. Since her life is "completely empty," she can fill the void with whatever she "choose[s]" (232), a discovery that leads to her considering giving a party.

She does indeed reverse the downward progression of her disconnection from herself and life. Smelling fresh baked bread, she "*seeks to follow the scent. The trail leads her higher and higher*" to the sounds coming from the kitchen, where a party is in progress. It is not a function requiring invitations, but a collection of personnel whose "*soft, friendly*" voices chatter as they prepare food for the patients and staff. Her discovery that they will be the company to whom she thought she would send invitations intimates a magical moment. "How I'm looking forward to supper tonight. Supper with the others up there in the kitchen" (233) are the closing words of the Lunatic's third and final monologue as she commits herself to ending her isolation and rejoining a community.

Scene 12, "Learner, Part III," again belongs to the Learner, who has yet to complete his task. The Lunatic discerns her place in the human community, the appeal of which is conviviality. In his garret in scene 9, the Learner discerned a "pattern in the universe . . . the heartbeat of the L" (227). The pattern is that just as L-words are limitless but limited by the initial letter, so the universe—of emotions, for example—is limitless but also limited by an overpowering emotion: love, the heartbeat of the human community. Discovering, as the Lunatic does, that there is an order in the disorder, he uncovered an order in L-words in which to express his overpowering love for the woman whose image overpowers him and who would, or so he thought, reciprocate. The task is incomplete because an "idea" (227) for an L-poem is not a poem.

In scene 12 he relates that his L-poem, read in the poetry course the two take, elicited the professor's grade of D+ and Lucheea's inattention. "It made me think . . . of other things," she answered his appeal for her personal, as opposed to the classroom, response. Declining his offer to help carry her books, she left him to watch her "walking, a shaft of light across her," out of the building and into a "burst" of "sunlight." In a play with allusions to Eliot's poetry, the shaft of sunlight alludes to the moment of illumination in part V of "Burnt Norton," the first of the *Four Quartets:* "Sudden in a shaft of sunlight."[12] *L-Play* ends with such a moment, with the Learner recognizing that he must continue the "eternal search of the word, the letter, the breath that would please her" (234).

The epiphany in "Burnt Norton" is that only in time is the timeless experienced. In love people experience Love, for the Incarnation, which is Love, is the Word made flesh, made love. The Learner's epiphany lacks the religious dimension yet is comparable. In the garret he discovered that love is limitless. In the classroom he experiences love for Lucheea so intensely that she is made flesh, for she appears in the scene to answer his appeal and to leave him. He and the Lunatic narrate their six scenes. The narratives are dramatized to the extent that although each character speaks to the audience, where possible he or she acts out what he or she says. In scene 9, for instance, the Learner is recumbent as he searches for an idea for a poem. The scenes nevertheless remain monologues. In this final scene, however, for the only time in the play, a monologue becomes a dialogue.

Learner's imagination, stimulated by his love, summons Lucheea for the recreated scene, and there in the sunlight, in contrast with the pool-hall glow on Shelly's face and the recommended striking of a match or shining of a light to check on an orgasm, her presence fires his imagination. What happens to him is also what happens to Carnelle. In the opening scene of *The Miss Firecracker Contest,* Carnelle records her "*ideas*" (147) about her talent-segment performance, trying to stimulate her imagination to yield the image of contest winner. In the final scene, after she relinquishes the false image, the "bursting" (204) fireworks flood her face with light. She yields, not to ideas, for she has none, but to the full current of her imagination. In the closing scene of his play, the Learner's imagination bursts as he sees the sunlight "burst" (234) through Lucheea's hair. His imagination on full current, love flooding his being, he too yields, not to ideas, but to the quest for images that will actualize the love, actualizing that will be his poem. The allusion unifies the play's scenes beyond the repetition of L-sounds to complete the play's design from the loss of love to its fusion with the imagination in a closing scene that reverses the midpoint scene. In scene 6 Wes wants to "get laid" (219); in closing the play, Learner wants to "please" Lucheea (234). His summoning her for the dialogue is a magical moment.

The allusion with its epiphany fusing love and imagination in a specific quest, the Learner's task, which is Henley's task, must be accomplished in a drama to which the playwright keeps adding incompatibilities and disconnections. She follows a predominantly verbal scene, a monologue, with a predominantly visual one, the scene with Shoe and the Ones. She alternates monologues as postmodern performance pieces with more traditional dramatizations, no matter how truncated, and in one instance inserts dialogue into a monologue. She intrudes surrealistic irrationality into naturalistic inexorability. By dramatizing fragments, she negates narrative as a structural device while interweaving repeated verbal and visual images throughout the fragments to create a narrative. A theater without incompatibility, however, would not be Henley's theater.

In an interview published in a newspaper article that coincided with the 1998 premiere of *Impossible Marriage,* she reaffirmed her interest in incompatibility as drama's matrix when she told the interviewer that the play investigates "many kinds of incompatibility." One kind is in tones, for the action "requires striking some sort of balance between deep, deep tragedy and foolish whimsy and being able to go from one to the other as kind of a hairpin turn."[13] These two statements indicate how *Impossible Marriage* develops from *Revelers,* which experiments with combining tragedy as a witness to suffering and reveling, and *L-Play,* which experiments with setting scenes solely through "lights, costumes, sound, style, and tone" (202). Finally, Henley's statement in the collected edition that the play takes place "somewhere outside of Savannah"[14] suggests that by setting the action somewhere between the 1980s Mississippi-Louisiana naturalistic settings and the 1990s Los Angeles experimental settings, she is merging the two creative periods.

The playwright herself in the introduction to the play identifies the first of the two stylistic and tonal influences on *Impossible Marriage.* Accepting a commission for a new play from New York's Roundabout Theatre, she wanted to write "something effortlessly brilliant with keen, incisive wit. Something like *The Importance of Being Earnest,* except by me" (xiv). The identification of the second of the two informing influences comes later, after the first is established.

The play opens in a country estate's garden, situated between the manor and the woods, on the day before a wedding; the estate's owner is Kandall, the mother of bride Pandora and her pregnant sister Floral. The first character to appear onstage is the bridegroom's son Sidney, whacking flowers with his walking stick and laughing, then exiting. When Kandall later rebukes him for kicking down a row of toadstools, she calls him a "foolish, stupid boy" (259). But Sidney is not the lone foolish, stupid character at the gathering. He has come to the wedding to warn his father, Edvard, that his mother will kill herself should he go through with the wedding. Yet even though his father "divorced his wife of twenty-three years and all of his children" (242) to marry the twenty-year-old Pandora, he does not recognize his son, who is in his twenties. "Perhaps he had a growth spurt," suggests the bride's mother. Edvard is willing to agree, since siring eight children complicated his life. "Seven" (248), Sidney corrects him. Kandall, the counterpart to Lady Bracknell, Wilde's society matron, has more than one line with a Wildean flavor. When Sidney tries to explain that he is not drinking so that he can keep a clear head to deal with his responsibility, she sympathizes: "I understand how confusing it often is—being rational" (257). Encouraged to proceed, he accepts a glass of champagne.

Although the obvious similarity between the two plays is verbal, as would be expected given Wilde's polished wit, there are similarities in visual image, in addition to Sidney whacking flowers, and in theme. In act 3 the pregnant Floral and Sidney share their anxiety about the imminent marriage, the sister because of her jealousy and the son because of his mother's suicide threat. Yet instead of acting, they share Sidney's muffin until Floral goads him into getting the pistol in the kitchen and shooting his father. Before he does, she orders him to "bring more muffins! The ones with raspberries" (263). The sharing aside, the scene recalls a delectable scene in the garden of another manor house, this one the setting for the Victorian farce's second act. Rebuffed toward the end of act 2 for not being Ernest, the two bachelors, Jack and Algernon, quarrel about their strategy for extricating themselves from their predicament while Algernon devours muffins.

Wilde's theme in all of his plays is the conflict between the desire for pleasure, which liberates the individual, and the conformity to conventional morality, which stifles individuality. With slight modification, the theme is Henley's as well. In her earlier plays, the conflict is between a character's desire for individuality and the conformity to conventional southern morality that inculcates submissiveness to male authority. In *Impossible Marriage,* the conflict is between primitive instincts and civilized responsibilities.

Accepting his responsibility to his mother by bringing her suicide threat to his father does not deter Sidney from yielding to his primitive instincts by whacking flowers. Neither is this occurrence the sole yielding to impulse. The play ends with Sidney declaring his intention to leave, now that the bride and groom have left, but unable to because he is with Kandall, together savoring her raspberries, though the fruit is not the sole reason for his lingering. When in act 2 the older woman refers to her first kiss, he kisses her passionately on the lips and professes his love. He declines her invitation to kiss her in the closing scene, but he is a mama's boy who calls his mother "M'amie" (249), and should she go through with her threat, he will need a surrogate mother.

Scandal is anathema to Kandall, who expresses her credo in the line, "Tradition cements our sanity" (266). The situations that develop during the twenty-four hours in which the action takes place threaten that tradition, or adherence to conventional morality, and therefore her sanity. Her immediate response to Floral's persuading Pandora to call off the wedding is to order the cake put away to prevent the town from "viewing it as an emblem of our impetuous hearts" (243). When Pandora has a change of heart, her mother dismisses Floral's suggestion of divorce because not only does it have no precedent in the family, it is "vulgar" (246). The revelation that Edvard's ex-wife threatens suicide should he remarry has Kandall speaking the dreaded word "scandal" and then repeating it moments later when Sidney threatens to follow suit with an "unsharpened hatchet" (253). The disclosure that should undermine her is Floral's confession that the child she is carrying is not her husband's, yet she does not crumble. On the contrary, she summons strength for Floral. Conceding that the scandal will be "monumental" and that all of them "will be raked over coals and publicly crucified without mercy," she is nonetheless psychologically prepared for it: "Oh, after all, who gives a damn?" (268). Reconciled with her daughters, she wraps a piece of the cake for Pandora, who leaves to wed Edvard in a civil ceremony, invites Sidney to kiss her, and savors raspberries with him.

Of the play's seven characters, Jonsey, Floral's husband, is the only one without primitive instincts, if dancing, which he does with enthusiasm, is discounted. He anoints "every crevice" of Floral's body but experiences "only calm" because sex "holds no interest" for him. In a Freudian slip that Wilde would have enjoyed, he admits to Edvard, "I'm that flaccid, I'm afraid" (255). Lacking primitive instincts, he has no difficulty maintaining civilized form. When Floral tells him that she must leave him, he announces that they will seek a divorce. The reason he gives, that he can no longer abide her snoring, is the stuff of farce, except that Henley is not writing a farce. Another stylistic and tonal influence informs *Impossible Marriage,* the examination of which must be delayed until after the examination of the conflict, the incompatibility, in two of the four remaining characters.

Floral sounds the conflict's keynote in the opening scene. To Pandora she attributes her irrational behavior the preceding day to her pregnancy: "There are cravings you cannot explain. These cravings are very deep and reason does not speak to them" (243). "An overwhelming craving" she "could not control" is her apology after carving a piece from the wedding cake and eating it with her fingers, prompting her mother's rejoinder, "Forgive me, I thought we were civilized human beings, not animals" (262). Pregnancy is a legitimate defense for her mood swings, with Kandall herself invoking it, but it is not the primary explanation. To mask his lack of desire, Jonsey pretends to be an ardent lover both within and outside his marriage. Hence when his wife experiences a mood swing that cannot be attributed to pregnancy or a sibling rivalry that has her interfering in her sister's wedding, everyone assumes that his increased attentiveness to her while failing to satisfy her need for fidelity causes, in Kandall's words, her "unbearable . . . behavior" (256–57). Yet Floral must share the blame with her husband because she too masks desire—in her case unfulfilled—by pretending to find the fulfillment she needs in their marriage. Hence when she cannot conceal the truth from herself, she experiences a mood swing, or, in the one instance that she went into weekly counseling sessions with her minister, the reverend, "for a time she seemed happy" (257). Here too, the words are her mother's.

The civilized form in which the reverend, father to her unborn child, sublimates his instinctive needs is his ministerial role. After his affair with Floral, he went on "something of a pilgrimage" to Nigeria (247), and apparently as long as he was away from her, he was able to perform his duties. Back home, however, and in proximity to Floral because of the wedding preparations, he cannot maintain the "hypocrisy." When he tells her that he "must leave the church," she tells him that not only is "penitence . . . not necessary," but he should not leave the church, just as she should not leave her marriage. Yet as they talk, each speaking the other's first name, they respond not to their civilized duties but to their primitive desires, and she urges him to "take" her. Touching her and then recoiling, professing his passion and then the impossibility of acting on it, the reverend so recovers himself that she recovers herself as well. "I never cared for you at all," she proclaims. "I am happily married" (259–61).

Neither exclusively farcical nor exclusively tragic, the scene closes the second act of a play that adopts neither tone consistently, though individual scenes emphasize one or the other. In an exchange between mother and daughter midway through the third act, Floral tells Kandall that the child she is carrying is not Jonsey's. To Kandall's question how Jonsey might suspect he is not the father, Floral has a surefire answer. They "don't have sex. . . . Ever" (267). If *Impossible Marriage* were Henley's version of a farce like *The Importance of Being Earnest,* this tone would persist to the play's end as Wilde's play treats the trivial things of life seriously and the serious things of life trivially from the opening scene to the closing line. Yet this tone does not persist.

In the introduction in which she identifies *The Importance of Being Earnest* as the first stylistic and tonal source for the play, Henley does not identify the second source, though there must be one to generate the incompatibility that is drama's matrix. She reinforces the notion of incompatibility when she writes that realizing her "characters' insides were vastly different from their facades," she tried to imagine the feelings expressed in Chagall's fantastic paintings inhabiting the figures in Beardsley's drawings (xiv). Chagall, however, cannot be the second source or influence because his visual images would qualify, with Wilde's verbal images, as examples of the whimsy in Henley's poles of opposition, quoted at the opening of the introduction to *Impossible Marriage,* between which the action makes hairpin turns: "deep, deep tragedy and foolish whimsy." The play's director, Stephen Wadsworth, provides a clue when he explains that Henley liked what he had done directing a Marivaux play: "What she wanted was a combination of things she had been drawn to in the Marivaux show: an envelope-pushing, heightened, theatrical style that was somehow grounded, truthful, very emotional" (xiv). The heightened, theatrical style is Wildean. The grounded, truthful, very emotional style is Chekhovian, particularly in *Uncle Vanya,* which is subtitled *Scenes from Country Life.* Though not a tragedy, the play has a tragic tone and thereby fulfills the requirement of Henley's other pole. Commenting on her play in a 1997 interview, she said, "It's Aubrey Beardsley on the outside and Chagall on the inside, or Oscar Wilde and Chekhov."[15]

The first act of *Uncle Vanya,* set in the estate's garden, introduces a theme that, like the theme of Wilde's play, informs the conflict in *Impossible Marriage.* Vanya feels that he has wasted his life serving his brother-in-law, Serebryakov, a retired professor of art whose deceased first wife was his sister. Infatuated with Serebryakov's much younger second wife, Yelena, Vanya drives her to distraction with his importunate pleading that since she too is wasting her life in similar service, they should be lovers. Although Floral in Henley's play will not be alone in realizing that she has been wasting her life, upon meeting the bridegroom, an artist, she confesses to the "big waste" (245) her life has been. Ostensibly to spare her sister a similar confession in the years to come, she gets her to see that she is marrying a man too old for her, and for the moment Pandora calls off the wedding. Chekhov's Yelena admits to Sonya, her husband's daughter by his first marriage, that she is not happy and wishes she were married to a younger man, yet calling off their marriage is out of the question, and she resists the temptation to have an affair with either Vanya or Astrov, the local doctor who is also infatuated with her.

Though each play has a scene in which a young woman acknowledges her unhappiness for having gotten into a relationship with an older man, the scene in *Impossible Marriage* between the two sisters does not invoke Chekhov's scene between the second wife and the daughter. A scene in Henley's third act, however, invokes not only a scene but a tone in Chekhov's play. As the ceremony begins, Sidney draws the pistol to which Floral directed him and, in a last-ditch effort to cancel the wedding, threatens to shoot his father if the others do not leave. Flustered by the reverend's undaunted approach, he accidentally shoots himself in the foot and falls to the ground. On the ground, he moans, "I'm such a failure, a failure, an abject failure" (265). In Chekhov's play when Vanya hears Serebryakov's proposal to sell the estate on which he and his niece Sonya sacrificed their lives and happiness to further the professor's career, he gets a revolver and twice fires it at Serebryakov. Missing him twice, he throws the revolver to the floor and slumps into a chair. In the scene that opens act 4 of *Uncle Vanya,* Vanya, his hands covering his face, wails, "I feel ashamed! If you only knew how ashamed I am! This feeling of shame is sharp, so much so it can't compare with physical pain."[16]

Eric Bentley finds that in *Uncle Vanya* the characters grow from ignorance to knowledge, and what they come to know is that they wasted their lives; they are unhappy because they failed to fulfill their potential as human beings. The effect of the professor's "visit is to confirm (as part of the general Chekhovian pattern) the fact that what seems to be so *is* so; that what has been will be; that nothing has changed."[17] Henley's characters also grow from ignorance to knowledge, but what they come to know is that they can change their lives. And they come to this knowledge, this recognition, because of the interaction the gathering forces upon them: making conversation, for example, or resolving crises. They therefore confront realities they have been avoiding about themselves and others. The difference between the interaction in Henley's play and in Chekhov's play is that the American playwright adds another interaction to the characters' interaction: she combines the grounded Chekhovian style and the heightened Wildean style in the three pairs of emotionally engaged characters.

When Edvard first appears, he seems to come into the play directly from Wilde's play, on his way to twentieth-century absurdity. Described as "*extremely appealing though decadent-looking*" (244), he is late because he was in a hotel fire that burned his cat and destroyed his documents, statements that qualify as the non sequiturs of theater of the absurd. Yet as the play progresses, he gains the agonized self-consciousness that would put him in Chekhov's play. The thought that his marriage might propel his ex-wife to suicide torments him. He also knows that he is too old for Pandora, described as the "*image of youthful exuberance*" (240), but he cannot resist the qualities she possesses that attract him: youth, innocence, and devotion to him. At least he tries to inject a realistic note into her romantic conception of marriage. To her profusion that their love "will last and last and last," he cautions, "Not necessarily. I mean my first marriage didn't last forever" (251).

He reveals the greatest depth of character in act 3. When he and Sidney first converse, he asks his son whether he remembers how he, Edvard, used to recite Dylan Thomas's poem, "Lament," when he was a child. Since Sidney does not remember, his father suggests he read the poem. In a play resonant with echoes,[18] such a suggestion should be taken seriously, and indeed the poem resurfaces after the abortive shooting when Edvard, assisting the stricken Sidney, recites the poem's opening lines. This recitation functions on several levels. Giving the stricken son something to do—and Sidney seizes the opportunity and joins in—it lessens his humiliation in front of the others. It reminds him of his bond with his father despite their temporary estrangement. And since the five-stanza poem images Thomas's ages of man, the older man's reciting is a gentle way of enabling the younger man to perceive that their different actions reflect the changing realities of their ages.[19] The joint recitation works; with tragedy averted, father and son are reconciled. Edvard also shows strength of character with Pandora. More than thirty years her senior and divorced with grown children, he has his "doubts" about remarriage, but he defers to her wishes because he loves her and because the alternative would be an unforgivable betrayal of her "newness" (269). He does not propose that they simply live together; he departs with her to be married.

Pandora's act-1 behavior puts her in the company of the young women in act 3 of *The Importance of Being Earnest*. When Gwendolen and Cecily discover their fiancés are not Ernest, they retire from the garden to the manor resolved to "preserve a dignified silence"[20] in the men's presence, which they break as soon as Jack and Algernon enter the room, the muffins consumed. Persuaded that marrying a much older man would be a mistake, Pandora leaves while Floral breaks the news to Edvard, only to come rushing back into the garden to embrace him. Kandall explains that Pandora "threw herself out of the moving car when she heard him shout her name" (245).

Plucking petals from flowers in act 1 or wearing immense diaphanous wings in act 3, she could be a flower child reincarnated from the 1960s. Yet she grows from innocence to knowledge to gain a Chekhovian recognition. In act 2 she rhapsodizes about marriage as a "wonderful state" (251) that nullifies loneliness. In act 3 she lifts the mask of the "lovely, joyous child everyone adores" to reveal a woman who, knowing that her beauty and charm cannot last, knows that nullifying the present for a problematic future would be a mistake. "Now is my time. I must take it" (268–69), she tells Floral.

The form that this takes subverts the audience's expectations. A flower child and a decadent-looking artist old enough to be her father would be expected to eschew conventional morality, especially since he feels "suffocated by all of this ceremonial paraphernalia" (263). But although they forgo a religious ceremony after the one in the garden is disrupted, they will be married in a civil ceremony, and not because Pandora is pregnant. In fact, she informs her mother and sister, she does not intend to have children. The simple explanation is that she is responding to her primitive desires, and marriage is a way of actualizing them. Henley does not take two free-spirited characters and convert them into something implausible by play's end. Pandora is still a twenty-year-old who finds romance in "running off to be wed outside the arms of the church" and who "*twirls*" with her flowers while waiting to depart with her man. Yet since they will be wed, Pandora and Edvard "*exit to the manor*" (268–69), which symbolizes cultivated nature or conventional morality, whereas the woods symbolize untamed nature or primitive instincts.

That Floral and the reverend are the second couple to leave should not surprise, once Jonsey reveals to Edvard that since he lacks a sex drive, he cannot be the child's father. The reverend is described as having an "*innocent aura*" (240); while undergoing counseling with him, Floral "seemed happy" (257); and the two are awkward with each other. That both rebel against a conventional morality they feel has forced them to repress their instinctive needs should not surprise either. At separate times they absent themselves from the others to roll down hills in the woods. She is the first to go, as she was the initiator of their sexual relationship. His apology for betraying her trust when she came to him for counseling she dismisses as ridiculous. "I seduced you" (260), she corrects him. Throughout the play she expresses her contempt for conventional morality. When he does as well by removing his clerical collar, they are reunited.

Where Henley surprises is in the couple's choice of lifestyle. They opt for a lifestyle that one would expect the flower girl and the artist to pursue. Even though she is going to have a child, Floral does not insist on marriage, and though he has been in the ministry throughout his adult life, the reverend is able to shed all vestiges of it with the removal of the collar. Committing his heart to her, as she commits her heart to him, he takes her hand and, in an echo of the closing lines of *Paradise Lost,* leads her "*out of the garden*" while "*gesturing to the whole world.*"[21] Consistent with the play's symbolism, they "*exit to the woods*" (271–72).

After their impassioned departure, the following exchange sounds affected, as if it belongs in another play:

> Kandall: Sidney, you have made a shambles of the day.
> Sidney: I've behaved abominably. There's no doubt. (272)

The dialogue could be Wildean, but the characterizations are not. Henley models her southern society matron partly on Lady Bracknell, but with such a change as to create a new characterization. Early in *The Importance of Being Earnest,* the Victorian society matron remarks to Algernon that his absence from the dinner that evening will destroy the table's symmetry, thereby forcing her husband to dine by himself upstairs. "Fortunately," she completes her sketch of him, "he is accustomed to that" (304). Lord Bracknell has a role to play only when his wife needs him; otherwise, he is irrelevant. After Floral reveals that she does not love Jonsey but stays with him because she wants to emulate her parents' marriage, Kandall reveals that she and the girls' father were not happily married but concealed their unhappiness for their children's sake. Rather than being irrelevant, their father was a man who "suffered" (267) with their mother, who continues to suffer—psychologically if not physically—because, as she confided in Sidney earlier, but has not yet shared with her daughters, she is hopelessly ill.

Henley is deepening Kandall's characterization until she is partly modeled on Sonya in the soliloquy that closes *Uncle Vanya.* In this speech, Sonya attempts to console her weeping uncle by telling him that although they have suffered on earth, they will be rewarded with fulfillment and rest in the afterlife. When Floral asks her for advice on solving her predicament of carrying a child that is not her husband's, the mother states her philosophy, beginning, "Eventually, we'll all be dead. Your travails will have ended and you can rest in peace" (267). Henley, however, does not continue deepening until the tone is tragic. She reverses direction by bringing Kandall together with Sidney in the garden.

Sidney is a would-be Wildean dandy who experiences a Chekhovian recognition. But whereas Chekhov's Vanya sees himself as a fool for sacrificing his life to serve Serebryakov, Sidney declines Kandall's invitation to kiss her in the garden because he is an "impossible fool" (272). That is, he wants to preserve the memory of their earlier kiss. She understands, for she remembers her first kiss, a secret the sharing of which emboldens him to ask for a raspberry. The scene succeeds in creating a Henleyan image that combines Wildean and Chekhovian moods as they "*stay eating berries together*" (273). That is why the lights come down on them. Just as the garden combines and balances the manor and the woods, so does the closing image combine and balance disparate elements present in Henley's theater at the close of the 1990s.

By naming the play as she does, Henley answers the question whether her union of Wildean farce and Chekhovian naturalism works. The marriage is impossible because instead of the interaction bringing the tones to full realization, the hairpin turns keep neutralizing them. The interaction of the two poles of incompatibility drives each character to a self-discovery or recognition of an unfulfilled life. The character's collapsing in the self's subsurface would release an introspective soliloquy, but Henley does not allow the Chekhovian element to develop. Reversing direction gives off verbal flashes, but no more than flashes. Gliding along the play's surface would release sustained wit, but neither does she allow the Wildean element to develop. If either element were developed, it would muffle the other, and she wants both elements. As she said about that time in her life, "I was dealing with how to live with polar opposites and not diminish either of them."[22]

The mix produces neither a purely Wildean play nor a Chekhovian play. It does, however, create a new kind of Henleyan play. If the only interaction were that of the characters, the play would be naturalistic and typical of her plays of the 1980s. Likewise, if the only interaction were that of genres, styles, or tones, the play would be a postmodern exercise. It is the combination of character interaction, Wildean wit, and Chekhovian confession that yields the characters' self-discoveries and their marriages, or unions, each more unconventional than the preceding one: an exuberant flower child and an older artist; a repressed woman who never had sex with her husband and an inhibited minister who apparently has not had sex since impregnating her; and a dying older woman and the virginal dandy who has his first kiss with her. These marriages are not only possible but pleasing. Take the most unconventional one. If Edvard, who is attracted to her youth and innocence, can unite with Pandora, who is attracted to his maturity, Kandall and Sidney should be able to unite too. Except for the servants, she is now alone on the estate and desirous of changing that part of her life left to her, and he needs the guidance that a mature woman offers. They can satisfy their desires and needs in a relationship the nature of which they determine.

In an interview in which she said that Kandall "takes a bit of a journey," freeing herself from the dread of a scandal, Henley explained why she moved the play's setting out of Los Angeles, the predominant locale of her plays of the 1990s. "I wanted an environment where there were more boundaries, where marriage was an institution that was valued. . . . I wanted an environment where there's an organized society for the characters to bounce off of."[23] To take up with a young man thirty years her junior, Kandall has to overcome society's perception of the appropriate behavior for a woman in her fifties and her self-perception as a dowager awaiting death. It is she who brings the berries into the garden and who, in a scene of self-discovery, recognizes in the conversation with Sidney about changing her life that "all the rest could be different" (272). When she then proposes that he kiss her, followed by an offer of berries when he indicates he is leaving, she is not proposing marriage. She is proposing an imaginative sharing that is both inside and outside the boundaries of relationships: inside in that the union is grounded in mutual love and respect and outside in that the two are released from the restraints of an institutionalized union. Since he stays, they experience a magical moment that hints at a union that can last, while undergoing change, until she dies.

The trilogy's crowning play, *Impossible Marriage* is also the crowning play of Henley's two decades of playwriting. It reverses the betrayal of marriage and the renunciation of love that open the second decade in *Abundance* and *Signature;* it is the counterpart to *The Lucky Spot,* which closes the first decade, in that both redeem the past. But whereas *The Lucky Spot* returns to the past to reunite the characters Sue Jack and Hooker, *Impossible Marriage* returns to the past to reunite the naturalistic characterizations that dominate in the 1980s with the experimental settings, styles, tones, and relationships that dominate in the 1990s. Just as Kandall took a journey to arrive at the closing scene, so did Henley—from the New Orleans of *Am I Blue* through the Los Angeles of *Signature* and *Control Freaks,* to arrive at the garden outside of Savannah. By journeying through the experimental plays to dramatize the discovery of the interior life freed from naturalistic restrictions, she returns to the boundaries of surface reality. The Lunatic in *L-Play* returns from her period of withdrawal from everyday reality by pursuing the scent to the kitchen. Henley does not return to the Magrath sisters' kitchen, but she does return to naturalism, though a naturalism integrated with spirituality.

Discussing the final play's final scene, Henley sees an image in it both confirming Kandall's movement from conservative dowager to liberated woman and defining a boundary that she crosses as a liberated woman. The image is "eating raspberries and letting the juice drip."[24] In statements like the one Floral makes about cravings so deep in a human being that "reason does not speak to them" (243), the play defends the existence of instinctual drives over which the human being has little or no control or understanding. Animal nature, however, does not wrest control of the scene as it does the closing scene of "Life," in which the Ones butcher Shoe in the blood-lust ritual, "*blood dripping from their mouths*" (231). By letting the berry juice drip, Kandall and Sidney are outside the boundary of repressed instinctual drives, but they let the juice drip in the garden: by accepting the spiritual gift the Ones reject, they also are inside this boundary. They are acting on their primitive instincts in a civilized garden; they are discovering imaginative possibilities for a sensual relationship grounded in love. Reconciling love and imagination, the scene reconciles animal urges and spiritual aspirations in an experimental interaction within a naturalistic setting. Much as Learner sets out to write a love poem for Lucheea, the trilogy is a love poem Henley wrote for the theater.

CHAPTER 5

Conclusion

It is commonplace in Henley criticism to relate her theater to southern writing, Chekhov's influence, and feminist theater. To relate her work to that of a few contemporary American playwrights with whom she is not normally compared yields new insights into her artistry. Her first important statements on how she writes excessive notes that get spread on the floor as the first stage in the creative process came in an interview of the 1980s.[1] These statements were expanded in an interview of the 1990s beginning, "I spend a lot of time filling whole pages of notebooks. Several, several notebooks. Then I work from the notebooks, and I'll figure out, 'Well, this applies to this character,' and put it under that character, 'and here's an image for that character, and here's a piece of dialogue that character might say.'"[2] The reader knowledgeable about contemporary American theater will recognize the similarity between this process and that of Richard Foreman. Although he has written extensively on how he creates, unlike Henley, who has made only isolated comments, the similarity is most apparent in his passage that details writing every day or every other day to generate material. "And I do think of it as *material*—I have no need to believe that I am writing *plays*. I came to understand I am just writing notes, thoughts, dialogue, fragmentary observations, some of which would eventually be staged." When he then gets the urge to make a play, he spreads the material on a couch or table and leafs through it, selecting pages that seem to have a connection one with another, "assembling the play in this very casual manner."[3]

Here the similarity ends. Although Henley admitted that her plays have an autobiographical dimension in that her characters are different facets of what she feels,[4] she is not writing about herself, whereas Foreman is writing about himself, albeit not the socially conditioned self, the circumstantial self: "Social life may focus our attention on character and its vicissitudes—and that's been the source from which most theatrical form has always come—but in my plays I want to evoke the deeper ground of being, the originating network of impulse, which precedes the circumstantial 'I.'"[5] The sentence's first part describes Henley's drama, and her theater in the 1980s is consistent with that conception. Characters on a representational stage look and act like people in everyday reality. The last part of Foreman's quote describes his own work, and his theater, naturalism's antithesis, is consistent with it. In a cluttered space that is not representational but isomorphic, performers portray impulses acting within Foreman's mind to create consciousness and theater. Yet the two are again alike in that they think of themselves as comic artists.[6]

Henley's plays of the 1990s do not resemble Foreman's work either, and neither do they Charles L. Mee's theater, though statements the two make about the creative process are again similar. In the preface to a volume of his plays, Mee lists the sources from which he gets the material for his plays: "history, philosophy, insanity." After an intervening paragraph in which he explains why his plays are not "too neat," he writes, "And then I like to put this—with some sense of struggle remaining —into a classical form, a Greek form, or a beautiful dance theater piece, or some other effort at civilization."[7] His *Orestes* is a good example: into the framework of Euripides' *Orestes,* he puts excerpts from *Soap Opera Digest* and utterances by serial-killer John Wayne Gacy alongside passages from the classical tragedy. As a result he can play the contemporary passages off the classical ones and the contents off the form to effect a re-examination of contemporary American values.[8] Twice in her statements about how she writes, Henley refers to the "chaos" in her creative process. In the late 1990s interview, she admitted, "I really work out of total chaos before I even start writing," and in the general introduction to the second volume of her collected edition, she characterizes *L-Play* as "fragmented and a mess" because there is too much "chaos to choose from."[9] She does not, however, put the chaos into a classical form. But not doing so does not mean that she neither experiments nor re-examines values.

In an article on Henley's and Rebecca Gilman's innovative dramaturgy, Janet L. Gupton distinguishes between socially preservative comedy and socially transformative comedy and argues that by experimenting "with comic form to supply their comic heroines with alternative outcomes" to those the former validates, the two women create the latter. The characteristics of transformative comedy are a group protagonist rather than a single one; subversion of linear narrative by beginning the play at the climax of the traditional narrative, as in *Crimes of the Heart;* heroines such as the Magrath sisters and Teddy and Bliss in *The Debutante Ball* whose transgressive behavior challenges the standards for femininity established by the patriarchal culture; and resistance to closure. By returning the southern woman to her role as the southern man's possession whose behavior redounds to his credit, closure implies preservative comedy, the goal of which is to restore or preserve the status quo. The goal of transformative comedy is the characters' recognition of themselves freed from an imposed identity and recognition of possible new roles for themselves.[10] Gary Richards clarifies what could be perceived as a contradiction in the way in which Henley alludes to her sources in the plays of the 1990s. As Richards analyzes *Control Freaks,* Henley uses her sources, Williams's *The Glass Menagerie* and Welty's "Why I Live at the P.O.," to parody in a postmodern sense the southern literary tradition in which critics have included her ever since *Crimes of the Heart.* That is, by citing canonical texts, she pays homage to the tradition at the same time that she spoofs it, as well as the regional identity from which she was distancing herself in the 1990s.[11]

Another apparent contradiction emerges from two statements Henley made in relating the emotional turmoil she was plunged into in writing an introduction to twenty-five years of playwriting. "Let the dead bury the dead" sums up her feeling about the past. Yet she also believes O'Neill's "observation that 'The past is the present and the future too.'"[12] An examination of David Henry Hwang's *Golden Child* can help to clarify this point. In a pivotal scene of the family's old-world history, dramatized so that the American-born Andrew does not abrogate his parental responsibility, his Westernized grandfather orders that the feet of Andrew's Chinese-born mother, Ahn, then a child, be unbound because foot-binding is an "outdated, barbaric custom."[13] The antinomy of bound and unbound becomes the play's central metaphor. Bound, Ahn is the repository of the past in that she knows the family history and awakens Andrew to his responsibility in transmitting it to his child, and unbound, she is the spirit of the future in that she appears outside the past to comment on the changes her father made and their consequences, two of which were her being the first girl in the family to "go school" and "choose own husband" (61).

The metaphor is central to Henley's characters too, for they are bound to the past—home and culture, family and relationships, secrets and guilt—and before they can become unbound, they have to return to the past, confront it, and accept it. They are never totally bound or unbound, though. Incompatibility and opposition are fundamental to her theater. Surrendering to the ruled surface or the unruly subsurface is not the creative way to live; reconciling the two planes of existence is. The same can be said for the playwright's work. That is why boundaries are necessary—in art as in life. The creative person has something against which to strive and to grow. That Henley is bound to a theater with recognizable characters in a unified, coherent plot ordered by act and scene divisions is evident from *The Miss Firecracker Contest* and *The Lucky Spot*. That she is unbound from it is evident from *Control Freaks* and *L-Play*. And she does create a new kind of play in her oeuvre in which she experiments with unconventional contents within a conventional form, one that interacts fragmented contents and naturalistic form. Yet her plays always retain the stamp of Beth Henley.

The personal identity of the characters in the plays may be another matter. In the modernist tradition, human beings have a true or essential self beneath the surface roles they play in life. This inner self may be lost, but it exists. In postmodernism there is no true or essential self, for existence consists of performing roles, and once human beings cease performing, they cease to live meaningful lives. Identity is fluid, leading to a crisis of identity, "arguably" the "most insistent thematic thread" in Sam Shepard's theater. Continuing to introduce the crisis in his theater, Stephen J. Bottoms writes that while much of the playwright's work explores a subsurface realm to discover the essential self, "there is also a recurrent fear in Shepard's work that the depth model of interior self within exterior appearance might in fact be a fallacy." Since there might not be an inner self, since personal essence might be a fiction, the "conflict between these incompatible depth and surface models of personal identity" is "unresolvable."[14] *Angel City,* in which a Hollywood executive and an artist switch identities, and *True West,* in which brothers switch identities, are two obvious examples of Shepard's plays that explore such a crisis. It is with the second play that Karen L. Laughlin compares Henley's *Abundance,* in which Bess and Macon switch identities. As Laughlin analyzes the play, it interrogates personal and cultural identity. For her, the closing scene "makes clear that fixed notions of identity as well as a clear understanding of linear history and purpose still elude" the two women.[15]

This book argues that the missing five years prepare Bess for self-discovery, but whether the self is the essential self or a performing self that is authentic only so long as Bess is performing on the lecture circuit is impossible to determine. Although this analysis also argues that subsequent Henley plays celebrate self-discovery, it cannot prove that the self discovered is a true, essential one. Sister integrates herself in *Control Freaks,* but not until the closing scene; the audience does not know what follows the integration. *Revelers* ends with the characters renewed by the evening memorial service and prepared to quest in new directions. Yet Caroleena's repeated "Poof" and the closing image of a sunset deepening to a "*multitude of unbearable, beautiful colors*" (198) hint not only at the impermanence of all quests but also at their conflicting motives. Learner's vow in *L-Play* to find the words to please Lucheea is an action predicated on his discovery of his inner self and his commitment to awaken Lucheea to her inner self. The play, however, ends with a recording of "*Dean Martin singing 'That's Amoré'*" (234), a song with lyrics so banal the image is self-ironizing.

Whether or not Henley's characters discover an essential self, her oeuvre's essential self is a theater that experiments while maintaining continuity with the past. "I think there are all aspects of human connections that I try to show in my plays," she once said.[16] The statement is also true for her dramaturgical connections. In a world of disconnections, of which she is ever mindful, her experiments go outside the genre's boundaries while remaining connected to them so that her exploration can test the boundaries in order to change or keep them. Created with love and imagination, the oeuvre secures Henley's place in the contemporary American theater.

Notes

Chapter 1—Introduction

1. The information in this opening paragraph is taken from Colby H. Kullman and Miriam Neuringer, "Beth Henley," in *American Playwrights Since 1945: A Guide to Scholarship, Criticism, and Performance,* ed. Philip C. Kolin (New York: Greenwood Press, 1989), 169–78, quotation on 172; and the front matter of the two-volume *Beth Henley: Collected Plays* (Lyme, N.H.: Smith and Kraus, 2000).

2. Haimes cited in Robin Pogrebin, "Sharing a History as Well as a Play," *New York Times,* October 11, 1998, sec. 2, p. 5.

3. Frank Rich, "'Abundance,' Beth Henley's Revisionist Western," *New York Times,* October 31, 1990, C15.

4. Beth Henley, *Signature,* in *Beth Henley: Collected Plays* (Lyme, N.H.: Smith and Kraus, 2000), 2:58.

5. Beth Henley, *Control Freaks,* in *Beth Henley: Collected Plays,* 2:112.

6. Gary Richards, "Moving beyond Mississippi: Beth Henley and the Anxieties of Postsouthernness," in *Beth Henley: A Casebook,* ed. Julia A. Fesmire (New York: Routledge, 2002), 44.

7. Karen L. Laughlin, "Beth Henley," in *The History of Southern Women's Literature,* ed. Carolyn Perry and Mary Louise Weaks (Baton Rouge: Louisiana State University Press, 2002), 588–93.

8. Julia A. Fesmire, introduction to Fesmire, *Beth Henley: A Casebook,* xiii.

9. There were critics in the 1980s who saw Henley's plays in terms other than those of a southern literary tradition. Two notable articles, for example, establish the affinities that *Crimes of the Heart* has with Chekhov's *Three Sisters:* Jean Gagen, "'Most Resembling Unlikeness, and Most Unlike Resemblance': Beth Henley's *Crimes of the Heart* and Chekhov's *Three Sisters,*" *Studies in American Drama, 1945–Present* 4 (1989): 119–28; and Joanne B. Karpinski,

"The Ghosts of Chekhov's *Three Sisters* Haunt Beth Henley's *Crimes of the Heart,*" in *Modern American Drama: The Female Canon,* ed. June Schlueter (Rutherford, N.J.: Associated University Press, 1990), 229–45. Today, however, studies that relate her plays to larger traditions in American and Western cultures are more common. In Fesmire, *Beth Henley: A Casebook,* see the sections by Rebecca King, Karen L. Laughlin, and Gene A. Plunka.

10. Beth Henley, *Revelers,* in *Beth Henley: Collected Plays,* 2:151, 165.

11. Beth Henley, introduction, *Impossible Marriage,* in *Beth Henley: Collected Plays,* 2:xiv.

12. *Mississippi Writers Talking,* ed. John G. Jones (Jackson: University Press of Mississippi, 1982), 182. Actress and writer Camilla Carr reinforces the influence. Introducing a volume of four plays, she writes that if Henley is to be "compared to anyone, it is to" Chekhov. Introduction to *Beth Henley: Four Plays* (Portsmouth, N.H.: Heinemann; and London: Methuen, 1992).

13. Jackson R. Bryer, "Expressing 'The Misery and Confusion Truthfully': An Interview with Beth Henley," *American Drama* 14, no. 1 (2005): 93–94.

Chapter 2—1980s—Naturalistic Plays

1. Colby H. Kullman, "Beth Henley's Marginalized Heroines," *Studies in American Drama, 1945–Present* 8, no. 1 (1993): 24.

2. Beth Henley, *Crimes of the Heart,* in *Beth Henley: Collected Plays* (Lyme, N.H.: Smith and Kraus, 2000), 1:63. Hereafter cited parenthetically.

3. Nancy D. Hargrove, "The Tragicomic Vision of Beth Henley's Drama," *Southern Quarterly* 22, no. 4 (1984): 55.

4. William Flint Thrall and Addison Hibbard, *A Handbook to Literature,* rev. and enl. by C. Hugh Holman (New York: Odyssey, 1960), 301–2.

5. Beth Henley, *Am I Blue,* in *Beth Henley: Collected Plays,* 1:73–74. Hereafter cited parenthetically.

6. Beth Henley, *The Wake of Jamey Foster,* in *Beth Henley: Collected Plays,* 1:124. Hereafter cited parenthetically.

7. Edwin Wilson, *The Theater Experience,* 3rd ed. (New York: McGraw Hill, 1985), 259.

8. Beth Henley, *The Miss Firecracker Contest,* in *Beth Henley: Collected Plays,* 1:165–66. Hereafter cited parenthetically.

9. Kathleen Betsko and Rachel Koenig, eds., *Interviews with Contemporary Women Playwrights* (New York: Beech Tree Books, 1987), 215–16.

10. Billy J. Harbin, "Familial Bonds in the Plays of Beth Henley," *Southern Quarterly* 25, no. 3 (1987): 91; Alan C. Shepard, "Aborted Rage in Beth Henley's Women," *Modern Drama* 36, no. 1 (1993): 96; and Larry G. Mapp, "Lessons from the Past: Loss and Redemption in the Early Plays of Beth Henley," in Fesmire, *Beth Henley: A Casebook,* 35.

11. Harbin, "Familial Bonds," 91.

12. Beth Henley, *The Debutante Ball,* in *Beth Henley: Collected Plays,* 1:307. Hereafter cited parenthetically.

13. Alexis Greene, ed., *Women Who Write Plays: Interviews with American Dramatists* (Hanover, N.H.: Smith and Kraus, 2001), 206.

14. Jonnie Guerra, "Beth Henley: Female Quest and the Family-Play Tradition," in *Making a Spectacle: Feminist Essays on Contemporary Women's Theatre,* ed. Lynda Hart (Ann Arbor: University of Michigan Press, 1989), 120, 125. See also Sally Burke, *American Feminist Playwrights: A Critical History* (New York: Twayne, 1996), 193–97.

15. For the order in which the plays of the 1980s were written, see *Beth Henley: Collected Plays,* 1:vii.

16. Beth Henley, *The Lucky Spot,* in *Beth Henley: Collected Plays,* 1:214. Hereafter cited parenthetically.

17. William W. Demastes, *Beyond Naturalism: A New Realism in American Theatre,* Contributions in Drama and Theatre Studies 27 (New York: Greenwood Press, 1988), 138–39.

18. Janet L. Gupton, "'Un-ruling' the Woman: Comedy and the Plays of Beth Henley and Rebecca Gilman," in *Southern Women Playwrights: New Essays in Literary History and Criticism,* ed. Robert L. McDonald and Linda Rohrer Paige (Tuscaloosa: University of Alabama Press, 2002), 124–38.

19. Hargrove, "Tragicomic Vision of Beth Henley's Drama," 55.

20. For Mac Sam's symbolic possibilities, see Larry G. Mapp, "Lessons from the Past: Loss and Redemption in the Early Plays of Beth Henley," in Fesmire, *Beth Henley: A Casebook,* 36, 39.

21. Karen L. Laughlin, "Criminality, Desire, and Community: A Feminist Approach to Beth Henley's *Crimes of the Heart,*" *Women & Performance* 3, no. 1 (1986): 35–51.

22. John Guare, preface, *The War against the Kitchen Sink* (Lyme, N.H.: Smith and Kraus, 1996), ix, xii.

23. Kullman, "Beth Henley's Marginalized Heroines," 22.

Chapter 3—1990s—Initial Experiments

1. Beth Henley, *Abundance,* in *Beth Henley: Collected Plays,* 2:4. Hereafter cited parenthetically.

2. Although he does not analyze Carnelle's recognition scene, Robert L. McDonald, in "'A Blaze of Glory': Image and Self-Promotion in Henley's *The Miss Firecracker Contest,*" *Southern Quarterly* 37, no. 2 (1999): 151–57, recognizes that "what happens in this play concerns a woman's constructive reimagining of what is possible in her life" (155).

3. Guerra, "Beth Henley," 120, 125.

4. Arnold Aronson, *American Avant-Garde Theatre: A History* (New York: Routledge, 2000), 9; Theodore Shank, *Beyond the Boundaries: American Alternative Theatre* (Ann Arbor: University of Michigan Press, 2002), 1–7; and Elizabeth Deeds Ermarth, *Sequel to History: Postmodernism and the Crisis of Representational Time* (Princeton, N.J.: Princeton University Press, 1992), 87–137.

5. Alan Clarke Shepard, "Aborted Rage in Beth Henley's Women," *Modern Drama* 36, no. 1 (1993): 107.

6. Beth Henley, introduction, in *Beth Henley: Collected Plays,* 2:vi.

7. Beth Henley, *Signature,* in *Beth Henley: Collected Plays,* 2:58. Hereafter cited parenthetically.

8. Janet V. Haedicke, "'A Population [and Theater] at Risk': Battered Women in Henley's *Crimes of the Heart* and Shepard's *A Lie of the Mind,*" *Modern Drama* 36, no. 1 (1993): 83–95; and Karen L. Laughlin, "Abundance or Excess? Beth Henley's Postmodern Romance of the True West," in Fesmire, *Beth Henley: A Casebook,* 88–104.

9. Greene, *Women Who Write Plays,* 212.

10. Miriam M. Chirico, "'Dancing on the Edge of a Cliff': Images of the Grotesque in the Plays of Beth Henley," in Fesmire, *Beth Henley: A Casebook,* 23.

11. Greene, *Women Who Write Plays,* 212.

12. Ibid.

13. Sam Shepard, *Buried Child,* in *Seven Plays* (New York: Bantam, 1981), 69. Hereafter cited parenthetically.

14. Stephen J. Bottoms, *The Theatre of Sam Shepard: States of Crisis* (Cambridge: Cambridge University Press, 1998), 162.

15. Ibid., 174.

16. Beth Henley, *Control Freaks,* in *Beth Henley: Collected Plays,* 2:112. Hereafter cited parenthetically.

17. Gary Richards makes the former judgment in "Moving beyond Mississippi: Beth Henley and the Anxieties of Postsouthernness," in Fesmire, *Beth Henley: A Casebook,* 51; Chirico makes the latter judgment in "Dancing on the Edge," 24.

18. Bottoms, *Theatre of Sam Shepard,* 160.

19. Ibid., 221.

20. Richard Gilman, introduction to *Seven Plays* (New York: Bantam, 1981), xxvii.

21. In a 1999 interview, Henley said, "Well, at the end of *Control Freaks,* Sister is empowered because she can finally be one person." Quoted in Greene, *Women Who Write Plays,* 220.

Chapter 4—1990s—A Trilogy of Experiments

1. *The Oxford Companion to Classical Literature,* ed. Paul Harvey (Oxford: Oxford University Press, 1946), 115.

2. For a capsule summary, see Bernhard Zimmermann, *Greek Tragedy: An Introduction,* trans. Thomas Marier (Baltimore: Johns Hopkins University Press, 1993), 9–12.

3. Beth Henley, *Revelers,* in *Beth Henley: Collected Plays,* 2:151. Hereafter cited parenthetically.

4. Charles Ludlam, *Ridiculous Theatre: Scourge of Folly,* ed. Steven Samuels (New York: Theatre Communications Group, 1992), 21.

5. For bringing a statue of Dionysus into the theater, see Arthur Pickard-Cambridge, *The Dramatic Festivals of Athens,* 2nd rev. ed., ed. John Gould and D. M. Lewis (Oxford: Oxford University Press, 1968), 57–60; and Zimmermann, *Greek Tragedy,* 10.

6. E. R. Dodds, introduction to *Euripides: Bacchae,* trans. E. R. Dodds, 2nd ed. (Oxford: Oxford University Press, 1986), xx.

7. Beth Henley, *L-Play,* in *Beth Henley: Collected Plays,* 2:203. Hereafter cited parenthetically.

8. T. S. Eliot, "The Love Song of J. Alfred Prufrock," in *Collected Poems: 1909–1962* (New York: Harcourt, Brace & World, 1963), 7. In a 1991 interview, to a question about writers that influenced her, Henley replied, "I love T. S. Eliot, but I wouldn't defame him by claiming to be influenced by him." Quoted in Cynthia Wimmer-Moul, "Beth Henley," in *The Playwright's Art: Conversations with Contemporary American Dramatists,* ed. Jackson R. Bryer (New Brunswick: Rutgers University Press, 1995), 122.

9. See Grover Smith, *T. S. Eliot's Poetry and Plays: A Study in Sources and Meaning* (Chicago: University of Chicago Press, 1956), 19; and Elizabeth Drew, *T. S. Eliot: The Design of His Poetry* (New York: Scribner's, 1949), 35.

10. Andrew Marvell, "To His Coy Mistress," in *The Complete Poems,* ed. Elizabeth Story Donno (London: Penguin Classics, 1996), 50–51.

11. Commenting on the influence of *Waiting for Godot* on her, Henley said, "I read Beckett in high school and it really was an eye-opener for me." Quoted in Bonnie Lyons, "Playing Dollhouse on a Huge Scale: An Interview with Beth Henley," in *The Muse upon My Shoulder: Discussions of the Creative Process,* ed. Sylvia Skaggs McTague (Madison: Fairleigh Dickinson University Press, 2004), 156.

12. T. S. Eliot, "Burnt Norton," in *Collected Poems: 1909–1962,* 181.

13. Robin Pogrebin, "Sharing a History as Well as a Play," *New York Times,* October 11, 1998, sec. 2, p. 5.

14. Beth Henley, *Impossible Marriage,* in *Beth Henley: Collected Plays,* 2:238. Hereafter cited parenthetically.

15. Lyons, "Playing Dollhouse," 153.

16. Anton Chekhov, *Uncle Vanya,* in *Anton Chekhov's Plays,* trans. and ed. Eugene K. Bristow (New York: Norton, 1977), 89. Hereafter cited parenthetically.

17. Eric Bentley, "Craftsmanship in *Uncle Vanya,*" in *In Search of Theater* (New York: Knopf, 1953), 348.

18. If one were simply compiling echoes of literary works, *A Midsummer Night's Dream* would be included. The season is mid-May, characters seeking relief from their frustrated desires flee into the woods, and Kandall rebukes Sidney for kicking down a row of toadstools because "fairies live under toadstools. Tonight they will have no place to sleep" (259).

19. The poem is appropriate on a few levels: the speaker's ambivalent feelings for his children, the "angels / Harpies" his "sunday wife" bore him; his contempt for conventional religious worship; and his adopting a strategy for dealing with encroaching death. The quotation from "Lament" is taken from *The Collected Poems of Dylan Thomas, 1934–1952* (New York: New Directions, 1971), 196.

20. Oscar Wilde, *The Importance of Being Earnest,* in *The Importance of Being Earnest and Other Plays,* ed. Richard A. Cave (London: Penguin Classics, 2000), 344. Hereafter cited parenthetically.

21. Cf. "The World was all before them, where to choose / Thir place of rest, and Providence thir guide: / They hand in hand with wand'ring steps and slow, / Through Eden took thir solitary way." *Paradise Lost,* in *John Milton: Complete Poems and Major Prose,* ed. Merritt Y. Hughes (New York: Odyssey, 1957), 12.646–49.

22. Greene, *Women Who Write Plays,* 202.

23. Ibid., 204–5.

24. Ibid., 204.

Chapter 5—Conclusion

1. Betsko and Koenig, *Interviews with Contemporary Women Playwrights,* 212.

2. Greene, *Women Who Write Plays,* 221.

3. Richard Foreman, "Foundations for a Theater," in *Unbalancing Acts,* ed. Ken Jordan (New York: Pantheon Books, 1992), 14–16.

4. See Betsko and Koenig, *Interviews with Contemporary Women Playwrights,* 218.

5. Foreman, "Foundations for a Theater," 6.

6. On Henley as a comic artist, see Betsko and Koenig, *Interviews with Contemporary Women Playwrights,* 216. On Foreman as a comic artist, see Richard Foreman, "Today I Am a Fountain Pen," interview by Elinor Fuchs, *Theater* 25, no. 1 (1994): 83.

7. Charles L. Mee, preface, in *History Plays* (Baltimore: Johns Hopkins University Press, 1998).

8. For a study of Mee's *Orestes,* see Robert J. Andreach, *Drawing upon the Past: Classical Theatre in the Contemporary American Theatre,* Artists and Issues in the Theatre 15 (New York: Peter Lang, 2003), 83–103.

9. The first quotation comes from Greene, *Women Who Write Plays,* 221. The second quotation comes from the introduction to *Beth Henley: Collected Play,* 2:vii.

10. Gupton, "'Un-ruling' the Woman," 124–38; quotation on 125.

11. Richards, "Moving beyond Mississippi," 44.

12. Beth Henley, introduction, *Beth Henley: Collected Plays,* 1:vii. The observation, misquoted, is Mary Tyrone's in act 2, scene 2 of *Long Day's Journey into Night.* When husband James exhorts her to "forget the past!" she replies, "Why? How can I? The past is the present, isn't it? It's the future, too." Eugene O'Neill, *Long Day's Journey into Night,* in *Complete Plays: 1932–1943* (New York: Library of America, 1988), 765.

13. David Henry Hwang, *Golden Child* (New York: Theatre Communications Group, 1998), 28. Hereafter cited parenthetically.

14. Bottoms, *Theatre of Sam Shepard,* 12–14.

15. Laughlin, "Abundance or Excess?" 99.

16. Mary Dellasega, "Beth Henley," in *Speaking on Stage: Interviews with Contemporary American Playwrights,* ed. Philip C. Kolin and Colby H. Kullman (Tuscaloosa: University of Alabama Press, 1996), 257.

Bibliography

Plays by Beth Henley

Am I Blue. Premiere at Southern Methodist University, Dallas, Texas, 1974.

Crimes of the Heart. Premiere at Actors Theatre of Louisville, Louisville, Kentucky, 1979.

The Miss Firecracker Contest. Premiere at Victory Theatre, Burbank, California, 1980.

The Wake of Jamey Foster. Premiere at Hartford Stage Company, Hartford, Connecticut, 1981.

The Debutante Ball. Premiere at South Coast Repertory, Costa Mesa, California, 1985.

The Lucky Spot. Premiere at Williamstown Theatre Festival, Williamstown, Massachusetts, 1987.

Abundance. Premiere at South Coast Repertory, Costa Mesa, California, 1989.

Signature. Premiere at New York Stage and Film Company, Poughkeepsie, New York, 1990.

Control Freaks. Premiere at Center Theater, Chicago, Illinois, 1992.

Revelers. Premiere at New York Stage and Film Company, Poughkeepsie, York, New York, 1994.

L-Play. Premiere at Berkshire Theatre Festival, Stockbridge, Massachusetts, 1995.

Impossible Marriage. Premiere at Roundabout Theatre, New York, New York, 1998.

Collected Editions

Beth Henley: Collected Plays. 2 vols. Lyme, N.H.: Smith and Kraus, 2000.

Beth Henley: Four Plays. Portsmouth, N.H.: Heinemann; and London: Methuen, 1992. Contains *The Wake of Jamey Foster, The Miss Firecracker Contest, The Lucky Spot*, and *Abundance*.

Three Plays. New York: Dramatists Play Service, 2002. Contains *Control Freaks, L-Play,* and *Sisters of the Winter Madrigal.*

Interviews

Betsko, Kathleen, and Rachel Koenig, eds. "Beth Henley." In *Interviews with Contemporary Women Playwrights,* 211–22. New York: Beech Tree Books, 1987.

Bryer, Jackson R. "Expressing 'The Misery and Confusion Truthfully': An Interview with Beth Henley." *American Drama* 14, no. 1 (2005): 87–109.

Dellasega, Mary. "Beth Henley." In *Speaking on Stage: Interviews with Contemporary American Playwrights,* edited by Philip C. Kolin and Colby H. Kullman, 250–59. Tuscaloosa: University of Alabama Press, 1996.

Greene, Alexis, ed. "Beth Henley." In *Women Who Write Plays: Interviews with American Dramatists,* 200–24. Hanover, N.H.: Smith and Kraus, 2001.

Jones, John Griffin, ed. "Beth Henley." In *Mississippi Writers Talking,* 169–90. Jackson: University Press of Mississippi, 1982.

Lyons, Bonnie. "Playing Dollhouse on a Huge Scale: An Interview with Beth Henley." In *The Muse upon My Shoulder: Discussions of the Creative Process,* edited by Sylvia Skaggs McTague, 145–59. Madison: Fairleigh Dickinson University Press, 2004.

Pogrebin, Robin. "Sharing a History as Well as a Play." *New York Times,* October 11, 1998, sec. 2, p. 5.

Wimmer-Moul, Cynthia. "Beth Henley." In *The Playwright's Art: Conversations with Contemporary American Dramatists,* edited by Jackson R. Bryer, 102–22. New Brunswick: Rutgers University Press, 1995.

Selected Critical Studies

Auflitsch, Susanne. "Beth Henley's Early Family Plays: Dysfunctional Parenting, the South, and Feminism." *American Studies*

46, no. 2 (2001): 267–80. The women characters suffer feelings of inferiority resulting from familial dysfunctionality, but although the plays begin in utter bleakness and futility, the women gain self-confidence and discover love and bonding.

Chirico, Miriam M. "'Dancing on the Edge of a Cliff': Images of the Grotesque in the Plays of Beth Henley." In *Beth Henley: A Casebook,* edited by Julia A. Fesmire, 1–31. New York: Routledge, 2002. Traces Henley's use of the grotesque from peripheral to forefronted as a means of developing character, as a subversive tool of rebellion, and as a way of forcing the audience to confront evil.

Demastes, William W. *Beyond Naturalism: A New Realism in American Theatre.* Contributions in Drama and Theatre Studies 27. New York: Greenwood Press, 1988, 136–44. Analyzes *Crimes of the Heart* as a fusion of domestic comedy and absurdist perspective with each character so expressing her own subjective order that no objective meaning or design appears. One survives by finding love.

Guerra, Jonnie. "Beth Henley: Female Quest and the Family-Play Tradition." In *Making a Spectacle: Feminist Essays on Contemporary Women's Theatre,* edited by Lynda Hart, 118–30. Ann Arbor: University of Michigan Press, 1989. Argues that although her first three full-length plays attempt to portray the female quest for autonomy, Henley's dependence upon traditional patriarchal dramaturgy undermines the attempt.

Gupton, Janet L. "'Un-ruling' the Woman: Comedy and the Plays of Beth Henley and Rebecca Gilman." In *Southern Women Playwrights: New Essays in Literary History and Criticism,* edited by Robert L. McDonald and Linda Rohrer Paige, 124–38. Tuscaloosa: University of Alabama Press, 2002. Examines *Crimes of the Heart* and *The Debutante Ball* as examples of Henley's experimenting with traditional comic form to give her heroines alternatives to the roles southern society imposes on its women.

Haedicke, Janet V. "'A Population [and Theater] at Risk': Battered Women in Henley's *Crimes of the Heart* and Shepard's *A Lie of the Mind.*" *Modern Drama* 36, no. 1 (1993): 83–95. Finds Henley's play regressive and antipolitically modernist when compared with Shepard's play, which is more postmodernist. Indicts the play for offering self-discovery rather than true liberation from the oppressive patriarchal culture.

Harbin, Billy J. "Familial Bonds in the Plays of Beth Henley." *Southern Quarterly* 25, no. 3 (1987): 81–94. Although loneliness, familial disintegration, and spiritual emptiness pervade *Crimes of the Heart,* the sisters discover the regenerative power of bonding. In Henley's subsequent plays of the 1980s, however, the characters are progressively trapped in hopeless resignation.

Hargrove, Nancy D. "The Tragicomic Vision of Beth Henley's Drama." *Southern Quarterly* 22, no. 4 (1984): 54–70. Studies both the negative and positive aspects of the first three full-length plays with the positive winning out in the dominant theme, which is that of the value of love and human solidarity.

King, Rebecca. "*The Lucky Spot* as Immanent Critique." In *Beth Henley: A Casebook,* edited by Julia A. Fesmire, 64–87. New York: Routledge, 2002. Interprets *The Lucky Spot* in the light of arguments by Hobbes, Locke, Adam Smith, and others as a critique of Western culture generally and liberalism and capitalism specifically, with gambling and prostitution as tropes for these ideologies and with the severest critique reserved for the family as the basic unit of society.

Kullman, Colby H. "Beth Henley's Marginalized Heroines." *Studies in American Drama, 1945–Present* 8, no. 1 (1993): 21–28. The protagonists of Henley's first four plays do not surrender to the futility and absurdity of contemporary life but instead quest for meaning, dignity, and selfhood.

Laughlin, Karen L. "Abundance or Excess? Beth Henley's Postmodern Romance of the True West." In *Beth Henley: A Casebook,* edited by Julia A. Fesmire, 88–104. New York: Routledge, 2002.

By reworking the myth of the American West through the genre of romance and thereby interrogating such concepts as personal and cultural identity, Henley creates a play in *Abundance* that is more postmodernist than are her earlier plays.

———. "Criminality, Desire, and Community: A Feminist Approach to Beth Henley's *Crimes of the Heart*." *Women & Performance* 3, no. 1 (1986): 35–51. Analyzes *Crimes of the Heart* as dramatizing feminine assertiveness and female bonding as alternatives to the self-destructive crimes that initially seem to be women's sole response to patriarchal culture.

Mapp, Larry G. "Lessons from the Past: Loss and Redemption in the Early Plays of Beth Henley." In *Beth Henley: A Casebook*, edited by Julia A. Fesmire, 32–41. New York: Routledge, 2002. Identifies the theme that unites the plays of the 1980s—the attempt by women to escape or overthrow the constraints of a southern patriarchal culture—and relates the theme to the works of other authors: Chestnut, Chopin, Hurston, Faulkner.

McDonald, Robert L. "'A Blaze of Glory': Image and Self-Promotion in Henley's *The Miss Firecracker Contest*." *Southern Quarterly* 37, no. 2 (1999): 151–57. Examines Carnelle's transformation from dreamer to realist in *The Miss Firecracker Contest* in the context of the changing role of self-image from Tennessee Williams's theater to Henley's theater.

Paige, Linda Rohrer. "Southern Firecrackers and 'Real Bad Days': Film Adaptations of Beth Henley's *Crimes of the Heart* and *The Miss Firecracker Contest*." In *Beth Henley: A Casebook*, edited by Julia A. Fesmire, 128–53. New York: Routledge, 2002. Examines the changes the playwright made in the screenplays for two of her plays, concluding that though she adds and deletes characters and shifts and rearranges scenes, she does not sacrifice her powerful themes of transformation and autonomy.

Plunka, Gene A. "Existential Despair and the Modern Neurosis: Beth Henley's *Crimes of the Heart*." In *Beth Henley: A Casebook*, edited by Julia A. Fesmire, 105–27. New York: Routledge,

2002. Argues that *Crimes of the Heart* represents Freud's notion of the modern neurosis, whereas the final scene represents the joy of unity that can counteract the alienation, loneliness, and despair that are the characteristics of the neurosis.

Richards, Gary. "Moving beyond Mississippi: Beth Henley and the Anxieties of Postsouthernness." In *Beth Henley: A Casebook*, edited by Julia A. Fesmire, 42–63. New York: Routledge, 2002. Traces the trajectory her plays take away from the southern literary tradition in which her writing originates to focus on her strategy, in *Control Freaks*, of parodying southern canonical texts to pay homage to them while spoofing them.

Rosefeldt, Paul. *The Absent Father in Modern Drama*, 75–82. New York: Peter Lang, 1995. Sees the world of *Crimes of the Heart* as a wasteland haunted by the sisters' absent father, who abandoned them, and Old Granddaddy, who filled them with self-destructive illusions.

Shepard, Alan Clarke. "Aborted Rage in Beth Henley's Women." *Modern Drama* 36, no. 1 (1993): 96–108. Traces the arc of Henley's heroines in her first three full-length plays from rage to rebellion to retreat back into the patriarchal culture against which they rebel.

Selected Performance Reviews

Am I Blue

Simon, John. "Slow Flow." Review of *Am I Blue* (presented with two other one-act plays under the title of *Confluence*). Circle Repertory Company, New York. *New York*, January 25, 1982, 56–57. The play has "both the promise of the lovely *Crimes of the Heart*" and a potential peril: a reliance on a bizarre cuteness associated with southern writing.

Crimes of the Heart

Barnes, Clive. "'Crime' Is a Prize Hit That's All Heart." Review of *Crimes of the Heart*. John Golden Theater, New York. *New York*

Post, November 5, 1981; reprint, *New York Theatre Critics' Reviews* 42 (1981): 137–38. This is a bona fide tragicomedy of three sisters stalked by tragedy with results that are comic. It would "be a crime . . . not to see this play."

Rich, Frank. "Beth Henley's 'Crimes of the Heart.'" Review of *Crimes of the Heart.* John Golden Theater, New York. *New York Times,* November 5, 1981; reprint, *New York Theatre Critics' Reviews* 42 (1981): 136–37. The play is a success and Henley has a prodigious talent because she lets the comedy develop naturally until it heightens "reality to illuminate the landscape of existence in all its mean absurdity."

The Miss Firecracker Contest

Beaufort, John. "'Miss Firecracker Contest': Beth Henley's Latest is Lush, Wacky Drama." Review of *The Miss Firecracker Contest.* Manhattan Theatre Club, New York. *Christian Science Monitor,* June 6, 1984; reprint, *New York Theatre Critics' Reviews* 45 (1984): 252. With its blend of emotional fragility and robust comedy in characters who are a blend of southern Gothic and kooky Chekhov, the play "deserves a life beyond its limited engagement" at the Manhattan Theatre Club.

Demac, Nancy Churnin. "Henley Play Bursts with Wit, Charm." Review of *The Miss Firecracker Contest.* Bowery Theatre, San Diego. *Los Angeles Times,* May 16, 1987, San Diego County edition, Entertainment sect., p. 1. Despite its similarity to *Crimes of the Heart* in parallel characters, the play is "most certainly a winner, even if it doesn't take first prize."

The Wake of Jamey Foster

Churnin, Nancy. "*The Wake*'s a Play That Deserves to Be Put to Rest." Review of *The Wake of Jamey Foster.* Hahn Cosmopolitan Theatre, San Diego. *Los Angeles Times,* June 2, 1989, San Diego County edition, Entertainment sect., p. 1. The play's fatal flaws are a "lack of focus and a lack of a burning question to drive the action." The characters' several stories remain fragments.

Sauvage, Leo. "On Stage: Dark and Shallow Visions." Review of *The Wake of Jamey Foster.* Eugene O'Neill Theater, New York. *New Leader,* November 15, 1982, 20. Although *Crimes of the Heart* and *The Wake of Jamey Foster* have black humor, the former is a success while the latter closed early. Some in the audience found the latter's jokes "tasteless."

The Debutante Ball

Sullivan, Dan. "All Odds, No Evens at the 'Ball.'" Review of *The Debutante Ball.* South Coast Repertory, Costa Mesa, California. *Los Angeles Times,* April 11, 1985, home edition, Entertainment sect., p. 1. The play has its funny moments, but Henley seems to be straining "for the next black, zany moment" because all the characters are so over the top that they wear down the audience.

The Lucky Spot

Oliver, Edith. "The Theatre." Review of *The Lucky Spot.* Manhattan Theatre Club, New York, New York. *New Yorker,* May 11, 1987, 80–81. A play about passion, it unfolds in Henley's imaginative world: "erratic, eruptive, and always surprising."

Abundance

Brustein, Robert. "She-Plays, American Style." Review of *Abundance.* Manhattan Theatre Club, New York, New York. *New Republic,* December 17, 1990, 27–29. *Abundance* (and Treadwell's *Machinal*) are examples of she-plays: domesticating tragedy into the victimization of women. Yet the plotting is "so random, the characters so arbitrary, and the theme so cloudy" that one wonders why the play "was written or performed."

Rich, Frank. "'Abundance,' Beth Henley's Revisionist Western." Review of *Abundance.* Manhattan Theatre Club, New York, New York. *New York Times,* October 31, 1990, C15. Although the play is the author's "most provocative play in years," it has shortcomings. It is more "patchwork" than an organic, coherent whole.

Signature

Klein, Alvin. "Hooray for Hollywood? More Like 'Horrors!'" Review of *Signature.* Mill Hill Playhouse, Trenton, New Jersey. *New York Times,* May 12, 1996, NJ12. The production can be faulted for overliteralizing a play the soul of which is lyrical. Henley, however, is "striking a blow for the reincarnation of the human spirit."

Control Freaks

Christiansen, Richard. "'Control Freaks' Deviates from Taste, Subtlety." Review of *Control Freaks.* Center Theater, Chicago. *Chicago Tribune,* September 22, 1992, north sports final edition, News sect., p. 22. The charming eccentricity of *Crimes of the Heart* and *The Miss Firecracker Contest* is gone. In its place are "deviant behavior . . . repellent imagery and dotty symbolism."

Shirley, Don. "'Freaks' Slips at End but It's a Fun Ride." Review of *Control Freaks.* Met Theatre, Hollywood. *Los Angeles Times,* July 19, 1993, home edition, F1. The play is undeniably funny as the audience gets to watch "crazies go over the edge." The switch to Sister's plight in the closing scenes, however, is too abrupt, with the result that the "ending falls flat."

L-Play

Siegel, Ed. "*L-Play* Is a Lifeless Lemon, Largely Lackluster, Leaden." Review of *L-Play.* Berkshire Theatre Festival, Stockbridge, Massachusetts. *Boston Globe,* August 28, 1996, city edition, C5. The play fails in every way. Take the characters: not only is there minimal motivation, "there's also no humanity in their development."

Impossible Marriage

Brantley, Ben. "Fairies Adrift in Love's Garden." Review of *Impossible Marriage.* Laura Pels Theater, New York, New York. *New*

York Times, October 16, 1998, E1. The conflict between "rarefied posture and primitive passion" is apparent in Henley's long overdue New York stage vehicle, but the action never takes the actors or the audience into the primitive world; it remains "stuck on the surface."

Index